The SOUTHERN COMPANION

The SOUTHERN COMPANION

Annette Spence

MALLARD PRESS

MALLARD PRESS

An imprint of BDD Promotional Book Company, Inc.
666 Fifth Avenue New York, New York 10103

A TERN ENTERPRISE BOOK

Published by MALLARD PRESS
An imprint of BDD Promotional Book Company, Inc.
666 Fifth Avenue
New York, New York 10103

Mallard Press and its accompanying design and logo are trademarks of BDD Promotional Book Company, Inc.

ISBN 0-792-45309-3

THE SOUTHERN COMPANION
was prepared and produced by
Tern Enterprise
15 West 26th Street
New York, NY 10010

Editor: Stephen Williams
Designer: Judy Morgan
Photography Editor: Ede Rothaus

Additional Photography:

21a, 86–87, 89 Ede Rothaus Collection, photographs by John Gruen; 27b © Runk-Schoenberger/Grant Heilman;
40 © Steven Mark Needham/Envision; 66 Ede Rothaus Collection, quilt © Stephen Blumrich/Pea Ridge Purties, photograph by John Gruen;
69B, 82 The Shelburne Museum, Shelburne, Vermont; 84–85, 88 Courtesy of Agnes Haward/photograph by John Gruen;
92a © Glenn Tucker; 113 © Christopher Bain

Illustrations by Judy L. Morgan

Typeset by: The Interface Group
Color Separations by: Excel Graphic Arts Company
Printed and bound in Singapore by Tien Wah Press (PTE) Limited

For my husband, Steve

CONTENTS

INTRODUCTION
8

SOUTHERN HOMES & INTERIORS
10

SOUTHERN FOODS
36

SOUTHERN CRAFTS & COLLECTIBLES
66

SOUTHERN GARDENS
98

I met a friend and her mother for dinner recently and told them about this book. Like most Southerners, they enjoy talking about the South more than anything else, so we spent the better part of the evening comparing ourselves to people from other regions. Eventually, my friend's mother tried to summarize by saying, "I think Southerners have always known they're different—they just don't know why."

That seems to depend on the person. If you were brought up in a home in which one parent was from Los Angeles, the other from Ellijay, Georgia, you're likely to be of the opinion that Americans can be cultural worlds apart. And in those circumstances, it would be fairly easy to discern at least a few distinguishing features between the two groups.

On the other hand, Southerners who aren't exposed to other life-styles and peoples may very well be unaware of their distinctive culture. I personally didn't appreciate these differences until I left the South. The first clue, of course, was how others reacted to my accent. I couldn't order an iced tea without calling attention to myself. And it wasn't just the way I said things that set me apart, but what I said. "Why, he is as mean as a striped snake" seemed to be a perfectly common observation to make—until I made it in an office meeting and treated my coworkers to a good-natured laugh.

The next regional roadblock was food. Hush puppies and fried okra are pretty much unheard of outside of the South, and I couldn't find barbecue, biscuits, or greens that

were worth eating. The trade-off was an opportunity to taste new foods, yet the everyday meals of home suddenly earned my respect.

It eventually became more apparent that the region from Maryland to Louisiana is like no other. The Southern home, for example, holds a unique place in American history: Witness such diverse aspects as plantations, the coastal architecture of Charleston, and the rise of the trailer park. Baskets, quilts, and brooms are crafted all over the country, but generations of Southern hands have contributed some of the finest examples— and are continuing to do so even as interest wanes elsewhere. Finally, it is here in the southeastern corner of the United States where lawn ethics and the traditional garden still thrive.

For all those who had to leave home to appreciate the South, those who make it their lifelong residence and have always been aware of its charms, and even for people who wouldn't call themselves Southerners but love it all the same, what follows is a sampler of this famous American region's claims to fame. There are more than a few generalizations here, but I've tried to present a traditional view of a traditional people and their ways. Enjoy what's left of it, because the South is changing by leaps and bounds—and has been for some time. Knowing these people, their pride, and determination, though, I would venture to say that the best South is yet to come. After all, tomorrow is another day.

—Annette Spence

SOUTHERN HOMES & INTERIORS

The sprawling white plantation house is only one kind of Southern home, although it must be the most popular and emblematic. Not far behind are the townhouses of New Orleans with their lacy ironwork and the proud old single houses of Charleston. When we think of Southern homes, these are the ones that come to mind—the ones we know from novels, movies, and travel brochures.

But otherwise, what is typical of Southern homes and interiors? We can conjure up images of screened-in porches and well-made furniture from North Carolina, but in modern times, Southern homes and interiors are basically less distinctive than say, Southern foods or trees. That's because Southern construction has been nationalized instead of regionalized since about 1950. Many critics blame air-conditioning for the loss of regional architecture in the South. With the hot weather under control, there is no longer a compelling need to include such features as shutters and verandas that once set Southern architecture apart from the rest of the country.

Whatever the reason, it is true that ranch, split-level, and other modern styles have been just as popular here since the fifties and sixties as in other parts of the country. It seems that the only contemporary home that could be considered uniquely Southern is the mobile home.

So any tour of genuine Southern homes must take the form of a romantic tour through the old South, except for a stop at a trailer park or two. Not all the old Southern homes were Tara-like mansions. To be sure, there are more modest Southern styles like the dogtrot, with its open central hall between two wings, and the saddlebag, which has a central chimney situated between two wings. These were built from the late eighteenth century into the twentieth century. Yet despite this range of styles, the South usually brings to mind grand porticos, weeping willows, and a long, tree-lined drive.

©Max & Bea Hunn/Visuals Unlimited

12

©Ken Osburn

*M*any of the great old plantation houses were torched by Union troops during the Civil War. Countless others burned down as a result of kitchen fires or kerosene-lamp accidents. Among the ones that survived: Montaigne, Natchez, Mississippi (page 10); Hay House, Macon, Georgia (left); and (below), this turn of the century house on St. Marys Island, Georgia.

13

©Grant Heilman

©Balthazar Korab

PLANTATIONS: KINGDOMS OF THE OLD SOUTH

Perhaps the strongest impression people have of Southern plantations was born of the fertile imagination of the writer, Margaret Mitchell. In her book *Gone With the Wind* she presented the saga of Scarlett O'Hara and her wealthy Southern family. When Scarlett's father, Gerald O'Hara, came to the South from nineteenth century Ireland, he made his mind up early that he wanted to be a planter. "With a ruthless single-ness of purpose, he desired his own house, his own plantation, his own horses, his own slaves," wrote Mitchell.

His incentives were clear, if abhorrent to the modern mind. Besides the "deep

hunger of an Irishman who [had] been a tenant," there was the status of plantation owners in the antebellum South. The government counted three-fifths of the slave population in deter-mining legislative representation, and about half of all slaves worked on plantations. What's more, taxes on slaves were generally low. And when Gerald O'Hara had the pleasure of meeting up with these planters from "moss-hung kingdoms, mounted on thoroughbred horses and followed by the carriages of their equally elegant ladies," he saw the same "drawling elegance" that fired the desires of others.

The contrast between a rustic slave cabin, like this one (left) in Baton Rouge, and the majestic homes of Natchez, Mississippi, is startling. Indeed, experts marvel over the paradox between the calm balance between life and art expressed by the white-columned architecture, and the chaos and inhumanity of slavery.

The Myth

But in truth, the idea that the South was covered with great antebellum plantations is more myth than fact. The exceedingly rich, slave-owning plantation dwellers who have come to symbolize the pre-Civil War South were actually outnumbered by much less prosperous farmers. Instead of defining a plantation's success by the pounds of cotton, sugar, or tobacco it produced or shipped, agriculturists used labor as a gauge. Therefore, we have figures today that show of over eight million whites living in the fifteen slave states in 1850, only four hundred thousand owned any slaves at all; fifty thousand of these possessed twenty or more slaves; twenty-five hundred had more than thirty. While this is still an incredible number of plantations that

exploited slave labor, it's fewer than myth might lead us to believe.

Plantations were not found all over the south, either; most were located on the Atlantic and Gulf coasts, Mississippi plains, and upland South. Between plantations lay many miles of small subsistence farms.

Nor were the slave quarters as quaint and comfortable or the "big houses" always as large and embellished as legend might have us believe. The truth is that cruel masters and crude shacks for slaves were far more common than homey cabins and benevolent masters. And though some of the main houses rivaled the enormous elegance of Nottoway—the sixty-four room white castle in White Castle, Louisiana— most began as simple log or board homes and were gradually enlarged.

16

©Balthazar Korab

Plantation Architecture

In fact, Tara is described in *Gone With the Wind* as having "been built according to no architectural plan whatever, with extra rooms added where and when it seemed convenient." In real life, only occasionally did a farmer build a house with architectural significance. When plantation mansions were actually designed, they were largely done in the Greek Revival style.

The white-columned style of Greek Revival homes was at first popular in both the North and South, since it was thought to be appropriate in a country that rejected its ties with England following the War of 1812 between the two countries. Then Southerners and Northerners alike came to see the style as a symbol of Southern chivalry, aristocracy, and hierarchy. By 1850, Greek Revival had fallen from grace in the North, yet Southerners continued to create homes with full-facade porches and gabled or hipped roofs until the time of the Civil War. Some plantation homes were created in the Gothic Revival styles, characterized by pitched roofs and pointed-arch windows as well as the Georgian revival styles, which included numerous dormers.

Nearly all were set on a hill overlooking a bay or river and surrounded by gardens, orchards, and trees. A distance from the big house stood the kitchen, laundry, and smokehouse, and further still were the cotton gins, rice mills, mule barns, sheds, repair shops, stables and carriage house, and the cabins where slaves lived.

A special feature of the Melrose house is the 11-color canvas flooring in the Great Hall. This 1845 brick mansion sits amid 84 acres in the famous "plantation town" of Natchez, Mississippi.

17

Preservation

In the early days of the Civil War, plantation life continued as normally as possible. The strongest young men went off to war while the women and hired overseers supervised the slaves. As Confederate defeats mounted, however, the plantations suffered. More and more rebel soldiers, even the very old and young, were sent out to replace the dead and captured, leaving the women and the slaves alone. Union troops advanced into the South, freeing slaves and robbing and burning plantations along the way. Then General William T. Sherman made his infamous march in 1863 to Savannah, wreaking even more destruction.

Like the fictional Tara in *Gone With the Wind*, however, some plantations were spared. A few were able to prosper again, operating with black sharecroppers instead of slaves, or

© Ken Osburn

© Ken Osburn

*N̄orth of New
Orleans, in
Vacherie, Louisiana, is
one of the most famous
and frequently visited
of the plantation
homes: Oak Alley.
There, 28 live oaks
over 250 years old
stand guard .*

bondmen. Others were deserted and
fell victim to vagrants or were used as
stables for horses and cattle. Nearly
all fell into disrepair until the period
from 1890 to 1930, when several
preservation groups and individuals
turned their hands to restoring and
memorializing them. The work goes
on today, so that Americans for many
generations to come will be able to visit
these remnants of the old South.

Plantations are notable for their
distinctive interiors. Here are
some classic components of
plantation rooms and verandas.

*A sampling of
antebellum
details, from left to
right: a four-poster bed
from the Davis House,
Montgomery, Alabama;
the sturdy richness of
mahogany furniture
in a Beaufort, South
Carolina home; the rag
rug, a still-common
sight in Southern
homes today; the clean
lines of shutters behind
richly detailed bal-
conies at Elms Court,
Natchez, Mississippi.*

Hassocks

Both hassocks and ottomans littered
the floors of antebellum mansions.
Apparently, well-to-do Southern men
were not only accustomed to putting
their feet up, but the voluminous hoop
skirts of the women were easier to
manage on these low, backless seats.

©Robert Perron

Elaborate Fabrics

At the wealthier plantations, windows
had heavy curtains made of brocade,
damask, velvet, or linen, lined with satin
or lace. The chairs, and settees (long
seats with backs and sometimes with
arms) were upholstered in leather, tapestry, silk damask, or embroidered linen.

©Mark E. Gibson

Four-posters

Beds with four tall posts at each corner
and a canopy overhead were popular in
colonial Southern bedrooms. Examples
of these may be seen at Melrose House
and Monmouth House in Natchez,
Mississippi.

Mahogany furniture

This durable but rich-looking wood
from the West Indies was used in many
pieces of colonial furniture. Varying in
color from light tan to dark reddish
brown, mahogany was ideal for the
drop-leaf dining tables, cupboards,
highboys (tall drawers with short legs),
lowboys (small chest of a few drawers,
used as a side table), and bed frames.

Marble mantels

Fireplaces were fixtures in almost all
colonial homes, and in the finer ones,
marble was imported for the mantels.
Scarlett O'Hara threw a china bowl
against a marble mantelpiece shortly
before she met Rhett Butler at Twelve
Oaks. Chretien Point, in Sunset,
Louisiana, has six marble fireplaces.

Porch chairs

Wide verandas were a familiar sight at plantation homes, and so were the wicker and slat-back rocking chairs that were set out on them in the evening.

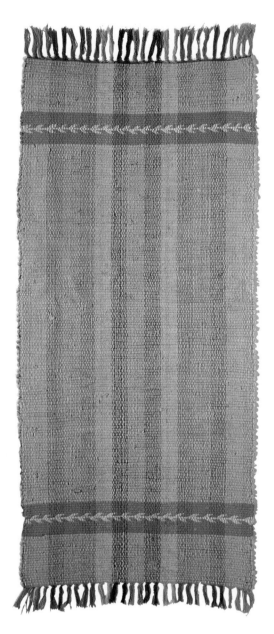

Rag rugs

In *Gone With the Wind*, Margaret Mitchell made frequent references to rugs that covered the wooden floors, which were dark and glossy with years of polishing. These thick, absorbent rugs were handwoven from colorful scraps of material.

©Blathazar Korab

Shutters

Particularly in temperate climates such as the Gulf Coast, shutters of wood, adapted from the marble shutters of Greek temples, were used on the exterior as well as interior doors and windows. Today, these shutters are enjoying a comeback as a window treatment.

Thick Walls

At Chretien Point, lunettes and fluted woodwork around the doors show off the heavy walls that architecture used to necessitate. Shadows-on-the-Teche, in New Iberia, Louisiana, for example, has 18-inch-thick walls; the interior walls of Oaklawn Manor, in Franklin, Louisiana, span sixteen inches.

©Mark E. Gibson

APRIL 1861
FORT SUMTER

Charleston's role in Southern history is more than architectural. In fact, South Carolina was the first state to secede from the Union in 1860, when the ten-year-old arguments between the North and South intensified. Following the secession of Mississippi, Florida, Alabama, Georgia, Louisiana, and Texas in March 1861, the newly inaugurated President Lincoln stated that he would hold federal possessions in the South. One of these possessions, Fort Sumter, lay in the harbor of Charleston.

On April 12, 1861, Confederate General Pierre Beauregard demanded the surrender of the fort, and Union Major Robert Anderson refused. It was Southerners who fired the first shots to begin the war that would change their world forever.

THE CHARM OF CHARLESTON

Charleston is the apex of a region that's well known for its romantic appeal. The city is rich in history and natural beauty, as well as in the homes that distinguish it from any other place in the South.

Founded in 1670, Charleston was named for King Charles II of England ("Charles Town"). Until the Revolutionary War, the city was the wealthiest in the South, based on large exports of rice and indigo, and on trade with Native Americans that extended to the Ohio and Mississippi rivers. Its location on a narrow peninsula on the South Carolina coast was so convenient and well established before the Civil War that Charlestonians found it easier to travel to northern coastal cities or to England than to inland South Carolina.

This link to England—and the fact that the first settlers were British—explains much of Charleston's architecture and furnishings.

Only a few years after settlers founded Charleston, they actually planned the future of the city. The original Charleston was confined to walls because the settlers feared the Spanish and native tribes. At first, the town had wide streets and large lots, but as it grew, more and more houses were squeezed in. The walls were expanded and eventually removed, but the tradition of building space-saving homes that faced the street and had self-contained gardens was established.

"Single houses," as they are known today, are unique to Charleston. Built flush to the side walk, these narrow houses are one room wide and have two rooms on each floor. ("Double houses" are two rooms wide.) In the early days, the homes were attached, in the northern European urban tradition. But that changed after the port of Charleston suffered a series of hurricanes and fires. In 1752, one storm

At first, Charleston housing appears uncommonly homogenous. But in time, a visitor realizes the city has many styles. These homes on Rainbow Row are good examples of attached buildings in the northern European urban tradition.

23

©Mark E. Gibson

89

CHRISTMAS IN DIXIE

Holiday decorating in the South is basically no different than in the rest of the country. Residents put ornaments and lights on trees, hang wreaths on doors, and light candles in windows. But America can thank Charleston for the poinsettias we've come to love, because it was a Charlestonian, Joel Roberts Poinsett, who first brought the red flower back from Mexico in 1828. Soon, others were decorating with the plant that eventually was named after him.

This classic old Charleston home (right) is typical of Battery Park, the peninsula city's southernmost tip. The houses here were built after 1820 and are newer than their neighbors inland. Before the Battery was a fashionable address, it was a marshland.

24

destroyed five hundred houses; a fire in 1740 burned three hundred. After this last big fire, most houses were built with spaces between them to keep future fires from burning out of control.

The extra space served other purposes, too. It kept the houses cooler and allowed for more elaborate gardens and piazzas, or tiered porches. Of course, the piazzas themselves helped cool the houses—they were usually built on the south or west side to shade the house and to catch the trade winds. The drawing rooms were on the second floor, since there was often an office on the street level.

The piazzas were not built all at one time, so the true single house did not arrive at a set period. Instead, it evolved; the piazzas were added to existing houses or included with new

ones as early as 1700 and throughout the decades to follow. Although historians point out that the original single or double house is English, the addition of the piazza can be credited to Charleston alone.

The City Preservation Officer estimates at least two thousand dwellings built before 1900 are still inhabited, and many of them are single houses. From Rainbow Row, a collection of well-preserved homes along Charleston's old waterfront, to the less-frequented East Side, where Columbus intersects America, examples of single houses are plentiful and varied.

In addition, there are mansions reflecting the changing styles of Georgian, Federal, Greek Revival, and Queen Anne, some of the most famous of which are on the Battery facing the

©Ken Osburn

city's harbor. Outside of town are the few antebellum plantations that survived the Civil War: Boone Hall, which still has the slave cabins on its premises, and the massive Palladian-style Drayton Hall. Restored or not, each home is a testament to the past, teeming with history.

The homes have been restored thanks to the perseverance and hard work of the Charlestonians themselves. Through war, development, fire, earthquakes, and hurricanes—one as recent as 1989 —the city's distinctive architecture survives. In fact, residents credit the city's tragic past for their will to rise again. And every spring, Charlestonians show off their labors with the Festival of Homes—they feel they've earned the right to be proud. Yet, as history verifies, Charleston has never been short on pride.

The city has a smell, a fecund musk of aristocracy, with the wine and the history of the lowcountry aging beneath the verandahs, the sweetly decadent odors of lost causes.
—Pat Conroy,
The Lords of Discipline

MOBILE HOMES: MODERN-DAY LIVING IN THE SOUTH

It probably wouldn't surprise any Southerner to hear that eight of the mobile home industry's top-selling states are right here at home—Texas, Florida, North Carolina, Georgia, and South Carolina round out the top five. The "trailer" as a modern-day home in the South has not only became a popular figment in our literature, it accounts for a substantial portion of our homeowners.

The trailer industry began in the 1930's, and it was then that the "home on wheels" first became a topographical American sight. The earliest mobile homes sheltered migrant workers and tourists and fell into the same category as any wheeled vehicle that hitched to a truck or car. But the terms "trailer" and "mobile home" became more distinct as the home became increasingly more comfortable. In the thirties, mobile homes measured about 9 by 6 feet; by the sixties, they ranged in size from 26 to 60 feet long and from 8 to 12 feet wide.

These days, mobile homes are rarely "trailers" and more and more are referred to as "manufactured housing"—especially since the industry officially adopted the term in 1976. They've recently been known to measure 16 feet across, and have expanded from the one-room, folding-bunk design of the early days to as many as three bedrooms, two bathrooms, a living room and a kitchen with all the modern conveniences, even a fireplace. Originally covered in sheet metal only, some present-day versions are skirted in brick or wood.

Perhaps the most striking change in the history of the mobile home, however, is its increasing tendency to stay put. The typical buyer of manufactured housing is not as likely to be intrigued by the mobility of the unit as by its economic value. A mobile home is not only considerably less expensive than a traditional house, but it also requires only a small plot of land.

Meanwhile the manufactured housing industry has grown into a multi-billion-dollar business since its arrival on the scene. For a few manufacturers, the market has slowed, especially when the largest units, the double-wide and multi sectional homes, suffered a drop in sales between 1978 and 1982. Still, other companies have continued to thrive.

Decorating with Collectibles

Your favorite Southern knicknacks can make the most attractive displays. Here are some ideas:

© Glenn Tucker

Pottery

Any collection of pottery is lovely, but even more impressive is a grouping of specific items—teapots or small pitchers, for example. The simplest way to display them is to devote a shelf or decorative tabletop to them, but one of the most charming ways to show off functional pottery is by placing the collection in kitchen cabinets with clear glass doors.

Seashells

Place seashells from a Southern beach in a pretty dish, acrylic box, or on mirrored trays. Plate stands are ideal for displaying the more unusual ones.

Books

For a casual yet sophisticated look, stack your favorite Southern books on the floor next to the coffee table or sofa or on an antique chair. Vary the books in size and content—a reference book, short story collection, a famous novel, and a glossy picture book, for example. Southern cookbooks from different regions are not only useful, they're a conversation piece for the kitchen. Display them with bookends on a countertop or shelf, or stack them on the refrigerator top (place a towel down first).

Candlesticks

Well-to-do colonial homes in the South featured plenty of candlesticks. Scatter them all over the house, or group them atop a chest. Don't forget to choose different kinds of candles and burn the wick slightly—an unused candle gives an effect similar to plastic left on lamp shades. Light the candles for special evening events. Candles burning in front of a mirror can be even more enchanting.

Pinecones

Collect pinecones in different sizes and shapes. Place them in a crystal bowl as a centerpiece; in baskets to stash in corners or in bookshelf nooks; or on the soil surface of potted plants. For Christmas, arrange them loosely on a tabletop with fat red ribbons and small ornaments.

SOUTHERN HOSPITALITY

For years, visitors to the South have been amazed by Southern hospitality. This graciousness is born of a long tradition.

In pre-Civil War times, for example, visiting relatives or friends might be welcome to linger in a home for months, since houses were large and visitors added variety to the slow pace.

As with so many hallmarks of Southern culture, however, there are misconceptions about the unquestioning kindness of strangers. Southern hospitality has not always been extended to people of all types. Southerners both past and present have been known to mistreat people of different races or classes. And in the outlaw-infested eighteenth century, just as today, Southerners wouldn't let just any stranger wander into their home.

Even so, there's no denying that, compared to non-Southerners, we're more likely to say "hey" to neighbors or strangers than people in other parts of the country—any visitor to the South will tell you that. And if you ever need help in changing a tire or directions to another part of town, you're better off with a Southerner than a Northerner any day. At least, that's what a Southerner would tell you.

©Russ Schleipman

The lower Quarter is the best part. The ironwork on the balconies sags like rotten lace. Little French cottages hide behind high walls. Through deep sweating carriageways one catches glimpses of courtyards gone to jungle.
—Walker Percy,
The Moviegoer

AT HOME IN THE FRENCH QUARTER

The architecture of New Orleans' French Quarter is not really French, but a combination of French Colonial, Spanish, Greek Revival, and Victorian. Most building before the mid-eighteenth century was done by the French who occupied the area. Then the Spaniards took over, and under their rule a few Spanish additions were added. But most of this architecture was lost when great fires in 1788 and 1794 destroyed much of the quarter.

The quarter was rebuilt during the early nineteenth century largely with mixed-use structures that had shops on the first floor and living quarters above. The French details persisted, but after President Thomas Jefferson finalized the Louisiana purchase in 1803, the more widely popular Greek Revival and Victorian styles exerted a strong influence.

Also known as the Vieux Carré, or Old Square, the French Quarter is characterized by graceful balconies that extend over sidewalks and patios behind houses, which can be seen through shady passageways from the streets. Dating from the mid-nineteenth century, these porches that extend around

the building at each upper level are American adaptations of the small and delicate wrought-iron balconies that extend under full-length upper windows in France. The enclosed inner courtyard was introduced after the 1788 fire, and made great sense in the tropical climate, as did the long, casement windows that reach all the way to the floor and the airy arches that are typical of Spanish architecture. The fountains, flowers, and leafy banana trees of these historic patios also provide cool relief.

Unlike some historical districts in other places, the French Quarter is a vibrant city. People still live, work, and play here as they have for over two and a half centuries. One does not have to search to find examples of eighteenth- and nineteenth-century homes, since these shabby yet charming streets contain nothing else —a visit is a step back in time. However, the following three house museums are considered to be the finest. They were all built in the years between 1826 and 1857 and are located within a few blocks of Jackson Square, where the colonial militia once drilled and public hangings were carried out.

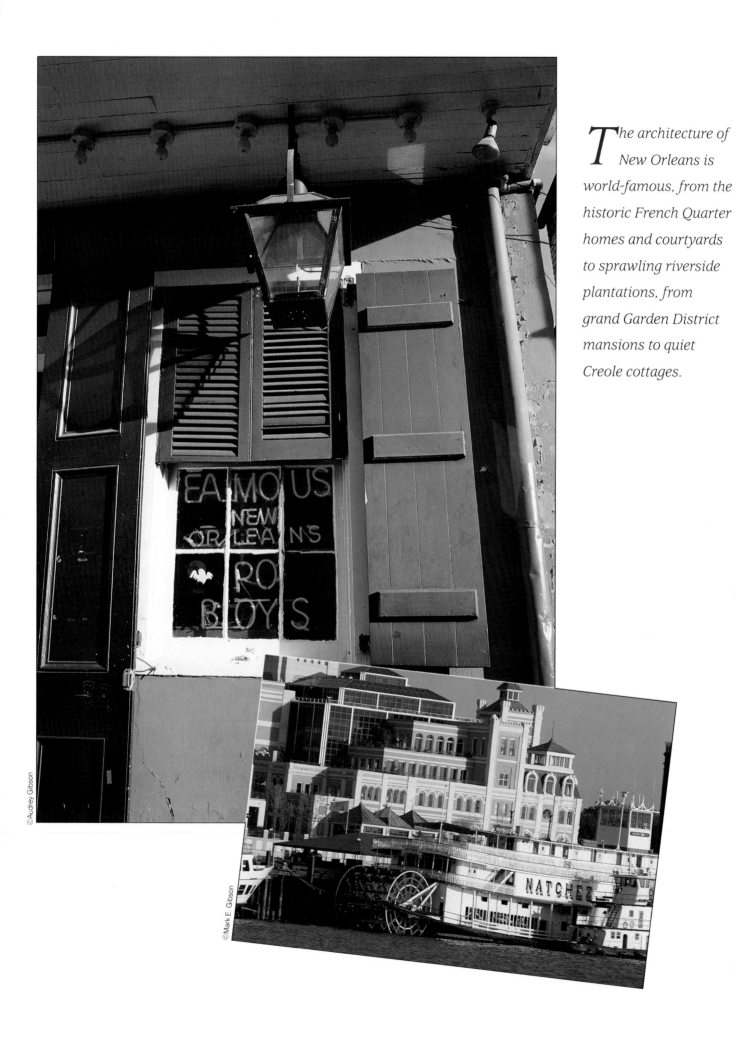

©Audrey Gibson

©Mark E. Gibson

The architecture of New Orleans is world-famous, from the historic French Quarter homes and courtyards to sprawling riverside plantations, from grand Garden District mansions to quiet Creole cottages.

29

30

Beauregard-Keyes House

The first of the trio, at 1113 Chartres Street, was built in 1826 by Joseph Le Carpentier, a prosperous French auctioneer. Le Carpentier wanted the mansion to be elegant in order for him to introduce his daughters to New Orleans' high society, and elegant it was.

Spaniard Francisco Correjolles designed the building, combining Palladian architectural elements with the raised-cottage style. The house featured a wide front gallery, white pillars, granite staircases, and impressive ornamental ironwork. Inside, the rooms had high ceilings, including a central hall with elaborate frescoes and richly detailed cornices, which was flanked by the drawing room and ballrooms. The dining room at the end of the hall opened through three great doors with fanlight transoms on the back gallery above the courtyard. There, a fountain was surrounded by tropical flowers. Black African marble framed the fireplace. The Le Carpentiers carpeted their floors in rich crimson, and though many Creoles used wallpaper in their homes at the time, this family whitewashed theirs to contrast with the carpet.

Despite their celebrated life there, the house isn't named for the Le Carpentiers. Instead, the dwelling is noted for two of its tenants—Civil War General P.G.T. Beauregard, who rented a room there after the war to look for a job, and the novelist Francis Parkinson Keyes, who took over the house in 1944. She furnished it with original pieces, including a rosewood half-tester bed and nightstand carrying the stamp of Prudent Mallard, New Orleans' most famous nineteenth-century furniture maker. When she died, she left the house as a museum. Her living quarters and study remain as they were.

Hermann-Grima House

Samuel Hermann was an immigrant from Germany who became wealthy as a commission merchant and married a woman of French descent. His house on St. Louis Street was constructed in 1831 by William Brand, and unlike many other homes of the quarter, it never had a ground-floor shop or business office. The house was also notable for having every modern convenience of the day (including a detached kitchen with fireplace, oven, and a slow-cooking potager) and scores of impressive details (fanlights and sidelights on the front door, matching second-floor door, and an unusual brass newel post rising from the bottom of a long, curved stairway, to name a few). What's more, the courtyard and entrance garden of this Georgian-Creole-style home are not only the most attractive in the quarter, but also the courtyard is one of the largest.

Hermann and his family sold the house to Judge Felix Grima in 1844. (Grima was known for keeping his horses in an adjacent stable—an unusual feature, since most French Quarter residents either rented horses for their carriages or boarded them away from the house.) Grima's family then lived in the house for five generations, until the Christian Woman's Exchange purchased it in 1924 as living quarters for single women. After the house was damaged by a hurricane, volunteers from the organization researched and restored much of the original house themselves. Today, the stables are used as a shop for antiques, handmade crafts, and foods, the garden has been stocked with plants that were popular in the period, and the rooms have been decorated with original furniture and paintings.

*T*he Hermann-
Grima house is
open to the public, with
shops, a garden, and
rooms decorated with
vintage furniture and
the original paintings
(this page). New
Orleans is still a city of
impromptu street
performances, wildly
contrasting colors, and
most of all, creative
energy (pages 32–33).

31

32

HOMES AND INTERIORS

34

Gallier House

James Gallier, a native of Ireland, arrived in New Orleans from New York in 1834. He had established a reputation as a major architect and designed the City Hall in Lafayette Square, which is now known as Gallier Hall. But when his eyesight began to fail, he turned his business over to his son, James, Jr., who became one of the most illustrious in a long line of New Orleans architects.

In 1857, James, Jr., bought a lot on the 1100 block of Royal, now a street of many notable homes, and designed and built his grand dwelling. Hot and cold running water, bathtubs, and skylights were considered luxuries, but Gallier wanted the modern conveniences and fashionable details of the day. To keep the house cool, windows reaching from ceiling to floor encouraged cross-ventilation, and air vents were installed in the master bedroom ceiling that let air circulate through the attic. The fluted Corinthian columns, elaborate plasterwork, and iron-lace-trimmed balcony distinguished it as one of the houses that replaced the French buildings destroyed by fire.

Gallier died in 1868, and the family moved out in 1931. The mansion became a boarding house with a barbershop in the carriageway, until 1965, when Richard Freeman and his family restored it, and then decorated it in a contemporary style. Eventually, the Freemans sold the house to a historical foundation.

Gallier was then redecorated in period style, and today it stands as a museum. The Victorian interior—with its original molded cornices and monkey-head motifs, cypress doors painted to resemble oak or walnut, and the summer slipcovers—is considered to be one of the most elegant and charming in the city, a testament to how people lived in the nineteenth century.

A well-worn saxophone awaits the master touch of a New Orleans musician. Visitors and residents alike flock to Bourbon Street and more out-of-the-way alleys to visit clubs where live music plays late into the night.

SOUTHERN FOODS

To anybody else, a Southerner has the same accent whether he's from Atlanta, Georgia, or Morgantown, West Virginia. But Southerners can detect a big difference between the graceful drawl of a Georgian and the West Virginian accent that hints of Pittsburgh. The South's foods are a lot like those accents. The cream-based chowders of Charleston aren't exactly worlds away but they're definitely miles apart from the cornmeal-crusty catfish of Arkansas. North Carolina and Georgia may be neighbors, but the boundary line that separates their barbecue sauces runs deep. And whereas New Orleans is known for the knock-'em-dead

glamour of its cuisine, Tennessee takes a backseat with its not-ashamed-to-be-plain cookery.

"People have said you are what you eat, and certainly Southerners feel a regional attachment to their foods," says Bill Ferris, director of the Center for Study of Southern Culture at the University of Mississippi, and coeditor of the Encyclopedia of Southern Culture. "Wherever you're from, the foods are considered a great source of pride." Crab cakes, for instance, are served all along the Atlantic coast, but Maryland often gets credit for the recipe. Smithfield, Virginia, and Lynchburg, Tennessee, are by no means large towns, but they're respectively remembered for their ham and bourbon. Meanwhile, Vidalia, Georgia has its onions, and New Iberia, Louisiana, has its hot sauce.

Yet, for all the differences among Southerners and their foods, there are also many similarities. Ever since the settlers took up the cultivation of corn from Native Americans, Southerners have been feasting on it in a variety of forms —corn bread, spoon bread, hush puppies, whiskey, and grits are just a few.

Turnip greens and collard greens are also rich in history, not to mention Southern identity. According to the Encyclopedia, *"Turnips were often planted in an open space near a pioneer's house site before he built the house," whereas collard greens are credited for keeping "General William T. Sherman's scorched-earth policy from totally starving the South into submission."*

Finally, the presence of pork in Southern cuisine stems from a time when most all Southerners were farmers and a "herd of swine" was a necessity.

Perhaps as much as anything else, however, Southern food is celebrated as a whole because we take food so gosh-darn seriously—"both at home and in restaurants," as Ferris points out. He continues, "The number of cookbooks that continue to come from the South is rather dramatic." At the same time, the very fact that we identify so strongly with our hometown specialities seems to peg us. One thing is clear: Food is foremost among the many topics that both unite and individualize Southerners. From both sides of the fence, here's a small sampling of Southern favorites.

Classic Southern foods include fried chicken (pages 36; 39), jambalaya and iced tea (page 38).

39

AUNT GRACE'S BISCUITS

So Jim he got out some corn dodgers and butter-milk, and pork and cabbage, and greens—there ain't nothing in the world so good, when it's cooked right— and whilst I eat my supper we talked, and had a good time.
—*Mark Twain,* The Adventures of Huckleberry Finn

When a person gets it in his mind to talk to Grace Hester about a particular topic, like biscuits, he ought to be prepared for interruptions. It's like talking to a ringmaster. Relatives stray in and out of the room, inquire of the whereabouts of Cousin Doug, and launch into colorful descriptions of old wood-burning stoves. Aunt Grace herself strays from talk of recipes to cotton gins to Doris' bad foot. And it's not easy to keep your own mind from straying back twenty years—to a time when you'd be out in the yard instead of sitting in the living room like a grown up.

Back then, Aunt Grace's house was virtually buried in Lithonia, Georgia, where there were trees to climb, scuppernong vines to hide in, and ducks to chase. Together with Aunt Grace's own offspring, nephews and nieces of three generations reveled in the good, clean fun of "the country" and Aunt Grace's home cooking. Today, her white house on the hill is about the only thing left of the little town east of Atlanta's suburbs. Now Lithonia is a suburb, teeming with the likes of her twenty-eight-year-old great-great nephew and his new three-bedroom house.

But all it takes is one swift hug from Aunt Grace, who recently turned ninety-three, to bring back those summer memories. The way she used to strip off her nylons to take you wading through the creek. The afternoon thunderstorms that got drowned out with cartoons and ice cream. The monstrous breakfasts that no ten-year-old could possibly finish but that she never made you finish anyway. And the fluffy buttermilk biscuits she turned out like nobody's business.

Of course, you can ask for it, but Aunt Grace has no definitive recipe. The proportions come naturally to her, just as the techniques do. But don't be fooled by an old cook's instructions— behind every casual detail lies a world of experience. Even though you're bound to gain a higher understanding of the Southern Biscuit, you won't achieve perfection by Aunt Grace's instructions alone. The average cook needs a definitive recipe (try "Christine's Homemade Biscuits," page 42). You'll also need time to practice—it takes about ninety-three years to get biscuits as good as Aunt Grace's. Here's her recipe.

The Wisdom of Aunt Grace

"Get you a big tray or bowl and sift in the flour—how much is according to how many biscuits you're going to make. For a small recipe, I'd say four cups of flour. Or six. You can use self-rising flour. I use it. But if you're not going to use self-rising flour you need two or three teaspoons of baking powder. And a little salt.

"Then put in some milk. Sometimes they rise better and are lighter when you use buttermilk. If you're going to make biscuits with buttermilk, which we did most often, you put soda [unless you're using self-rising flour, which already has soda]. If you don't have buttermilk you better not put the soda. You can use a little sweet milk or any kind of milk you have, but I wouldn't use water. I wouldn't think of trying to make them without buttermilk or sweet milk.

"Then you've got to put some lard, some shortening, in there. Crisco, that's what I use. Mix it all up with your fingers as you go. Get down and knead it. Get your flour all in where you can pick it up, but don't mix it too much. Make the dough stiff enough so it will roll without sticking to your roller but soft enough so you can handle it. When it's soft and rolled in flour—not wet—put the dough out on your board.

"Roll the dough smooth. No, you don't want to roll them too thin. Or too thick. About an inch. And take your biscuit cutter and cut it. Have your pan greased, a big pan that you're going to cook the biscuits in. And take the biscuits off the board and put them in the pan.

"The temperature, its according to your stove. I'd say about 300 degrees, 350 degrees. Ten minutes or so if your stove's hot, but you'll have to judge that. When they rise—they'll rise—and begin to brown, they're getting done. You better watch them. Golden brown on top. If they're golden brown on top —and your stove's alright—then they'll be alright on the bottom, too. Yes, you can do it. It's not hard."

GREATEST BISCUIT HITS

The Southern biscuit varies a little from table to table. It can be sweeter, saltier, more buttery, bigger, softer, or slightly crunchier. But any time Southerners ask for biscuits, they generally know what food to expect. Because a biscuit should not only be round, feathery, and light with a moist interior and a crusty brown top, it should also be adaptable.

For example, you should be able to split a couple of biscuits in the middle and then pile them high with gravy. Biscuits and gravy, like most biscuit combinations, are old standards at breakfast, but they've been known to pop up at most any meal.

Any time you're blessed with both a plate of biscuits and country sausage or ham on the table, you'd be crazy not to make a ham biscuit or sausage biscuit. A Massachusetts resident once asked if a ham biscuit had ham chopped up and suspended in the biscuit dough. It's not that complicated. A ham or sausage biscuit is just a sandwich: a split biscuit with a slice of country ham or a sausage patty stuck in the middle. Fast-food restaurants have had a field day with this notion, so that now the chicken biscuit and steak biscuit are almost as popular.

The biscuit is also a wonderful ingredient for dressing (crumbled together with corn bread and sausage); strawberry shortcakes (split and heaped with sugared berries in the middle, topped with more berries and whipped cream); and other dessert combinations (smothered in apple-sauce and brown sugar or baked on top of fruit cobbler). They've even been known to serve as chicken feed—but only way after breakfast, when they get cold and hard.

If a biscuit can meet all these functions, it's pretty well-rounded. But, above all, a Southern biscuit has to stand on its own with a little sweet butter, apple butter, honey, or (best yet) all by itself.

Christine's Homemade Biscuits

If you'd like a recipe that's a little more specific than Aunt Grace's, try this one. Customers at the Gardens Restaurant in Pine Mountain, Georgia, enjoy Christine Copeland's biscuits at every meal.

5 cups all-purpose flour

6 tablespoons baking powder

2 teaspoons salt

2 tablespoons sugar

1 cup shortening

2 cups buttermilk

In a large bowl, sift together flour, baking powder, salt, and sugar. Stir until mixed well. Dig a hole in the center of this mixture with the side of your hand. Put the shortening in this hole and, while gradually adding buttermilk, mix it all together to form a soft dough batter.

Knead soft dough and flour from the side of the bowl to form a roll. Sprinkle flour on your hands and pinch off small pieces of dough. Roll pieces of dough in the palms of your hands to form balls.

Place on a greased sheet pan and flatten the dough balls slightly to form a nice circle. Bake at 325 degrees until slightly brown.

Makes 15 biscuits

Milk Gravy

Though gravy does nothing to increase life spans, Southerners still can't resist ladling it over meats and biscuits. Milk gravy is good with sausage, cube steak, and fried chicken. Using the same method, you can also make Red-Eye Gravy (with a few tablespoons of coffee and about 1/3 cup of water) to complement country ham.

2 to 3 tablespoons cooking fat from sausage, chicken or cubesteak

1 cup milk

1 cup water

2 tablespoons flour

Salt and pepper

Combine milk and water in a small bowl. Fry meat in pan, then pour off all but 2 to 3 tablespoons fat. Over low heat, add flour and make a paste with the fat, stirring constantly to prevent burning and to scrape up any small bits of meat. Add about a fourth of the milk-water mixture while continuing to stir.

When the gravy thickens slightly, gradually add the rest of the milk-water mixture. Once all the milk-water mixture is stirred in, allow the gravy to simmer for a minute or two, until it reaches the desired consistency. Season to taste with salt and pepper.

Serves 4

Southern Sausage

Slice off 1/2- to 1-inch patties of ground sausage. In a skillet over medium heat, fry the patties for 15 to 20 minutes, turning once, until patties are brown and no pinkness remains. Drain on paper towels and serve.

Country Ham

Slice country-style ham into 1/4-inch slices, and then cut them in half if they're bigger than 1 serving. Score the fatty edges to prevent curling.

In a heavy skillet over medium heat, fry the pieces slowly, turning frequently. Cook about 10 minutes, until both sides are very lightly browned.

Some Southerners like to sprinkle on brown sugar as the ham fries, to add flavor and color.

Grits

Made from the ground dried hulls of corn kernels (hominy), grits are often served at breakfast along with bacon, ham, or sausage; fried or scrambled eggs; gravy and biscuits; and sometimes fried apples, tomatoes, or potatoes. At other meals grits can be fried in bacon grease or baked with cheese and garlic, but in the morning they're best as a porridge with a little butter and sugar mixed in or topped with gravy.

Homemade Grits

3 cups water

1/4 teaspoon salt

3/4 to 1 cup grits

Bring the water and salt to a boil in a heavy saucepan. Stir in the grits, using more grits if you like them thick. Continue to stir and cook over medium heat until grits taste done and are thick, about 20 minutes.

Remove from heat, cover, and let stand and thicken some more for a few minutes.

Serves 4

44

FOODS

FOODS

*S*outhern barbecue varies from state to state, town to town, family to family. In Texas, barbecue is barbecued beef ribs; in North Carolina, it's most likely to be chopped pork roast soaked in savory sauce.

46

THE BARBECUE DISPUTE

Steve Bender was what you might call nouveau Southern when he experienced his first barbecue dispute. After twenty-two years in Indiana and six years in New York City, he was just getting the hang of a new life in North Carolina when he stopped off for barbecue one night. The waitress brought him a plate of sliced pork roast beneath a trail of sweet, rust-colored sauce. Steve was livid. "This isn't barbecue!" he scolded. The waitress apologized, substituted a hamburger, and later, over a cigarette, dismissed him as a damn Yankee.

Actually, Steve was behaving more like a Southerner than he, or the waitress, realized. That's because he had already come to love a barbecue that was smoked, chopped, and soaked with a spicy, orange-colored sauce. True, a Southerner would have realized that barbecue varies from restaurant to restaurant, and a Southerner would have called the waitress "Ma'am" instead of "Miss." But you can't blame the man for liking his barbecue.

There are a few distinguishing barbecue features that draw Southerners together, yet there are a whole lot more that pull them apart. "Barbecue has become a symbolic food not only for the Southern region itself but also for its subregions," says Bill Ferris, director of The Center for Study of Southern Culture at the University of Mississippi and coeditor of the *Encyclopedia of Southern Culture.* "There are competitions and very emotional arguments over what is the true and best barbecue."

Now, for the most part, Southerners do agree that barbecue should be used as a noun—not a verb, as it is used in other parts of the country—and that barbecue is cooked slowly over wood smoke in brick ovens, pits, or metal drum-like smokers. Finally, barbecue should have a memorable sauce. (Most Southerners will at least go along with this last point.)

But from that point on opinions scatter like chickens. Take the meat. In Texas (which is normally considered to be in the Southwest, except when it comes to barbecue), beef ribs are a must. In the Southeast—particularly the Carolinas, Alabama, Georgia, Tennessee, and Mississippi—pork is the only way to go. Of course, there's also room for specialties: Mississippians, for example, have been known to barbecue a goat on holidays, and Kentuckians have a taste for barbecued mutton.

When the conversation turns to sauce, sparks fly. The main argument is between the spicy, vinegar-based sauce of eastern North Carolina and the sweet, tomato-based sauce of Georgia and the rest of the deep South. Even so a few South Carolinians hold that a tangy, mustard-based sauce could lick the others any day. Furthermore, there are all sorts of theories on whether it's best to add the sauce before, during, or after the meat has cooked; to slice, chop, or pull the pork off the bone; what sort of wood has the best flavor; and so on.

What's a barbecuer to do? Some restaurants offer a choice of sauces and meats—and barbecued chicken to boot. Others, like Dreamland Drive Inn Bar-B-Q in Tuscaloosa, Alabama, feature one type of barbecue. John Bishop wouldn't dream of compromising his values. For thirty-some years, Bishop has served the same sauce and the same menu: ribs, chips, and white bread. And he doesn't care about the competition.

Although he's been courted by the likes of the *New York Times* and *Southern Magazine*, Bishop doesn't care to give away his sauce recipe, either. ("Wouldn't be no need to come out here then.") Which is no surprise, since getting a barbecue recipe out of a Southerner is like getting blood from a turnip.

"Our formula? Oh no, we can't tell you that," says Lise King, wife of the owner of Carolina Treet, a bottled sauce based in Wilmington, North Carolina. The sentiments are the same wherever you turn. "I've given out other recipes," says Tom Seaton, owner of Firehouse Barbecue in Johnson City, Tennessee, "but I still hold the sauces dear."

Never mind. For all the passion and secretiveness that barbecue provokes among Southerners, it seems to be a good-natured rivalry. At least we all agree on which state invented barbecue. Or do we?

"Well, I think you'd find that claim from just about every region," says Ferris. You see, on the one hand there's this argument that…

I don't know about any other barbecue and I don't eat nobody else's.
—John Bishop, owner of Dreamland Drive Inn Bar-B-Q, Tuscaloosa, Alabama

47

Basic Tomato-Based Barbecue Sauce

The sweeter sauces often include the following ingredients (give or take some spices): garlic, oil, tomato sauce, and celery. Furthermore, the recipe changes depending on who is making the sauce. The idea is to start with the basics here and dabble until you get the proportions that suit your own taste.

1 cup onion, finely chopped

2 tablespoons margarine

1/4 cup cider vinegar

1/4 cup Worcestershire sauce

1/4 cup brown sugar

2 tablespoons lemon juice

1/2 teaspoon dry mustard

2 cups ketchup

1 cup water

Salt and black pepper to taste

Crushed red pepper to taste

In a large saucepan, cook onion in margarine until browned. Add the remaining ingredients, bring to a boil, and simmer at least 45 minutes, stirring occasionally. Adjust seasonings to taste.

Makes 5 cups of sauce, enough for about 3 cups chopped meat or more than enough for grilling 5 pounds of chicken or pork.

Basic Vinegar-Based Sauce

Unlike the thick, condiment-style tomato sauces, the vinegar-and-pepper sauces are runny and best suited for basting on the grill or drizzling on a mess of chopped, smoked meat. Once again, every recipe varies but here's a starting point.

2 cups cider vinegar

1 cup margarine, melted

1 tablespoon lemon juice

Dash Worcestershire sauce

Crushed red pepper and salt to taste

In a medium saucepan, combine all ingredients. Heat to just below the boiling point and simmer for 30 minutes or so. Leftover sauce may be refrigerated.

Makes 3 cups

Coleslaw

The word comes from *kool* and *sla*, Dutch words for cabbage and salad, respectfully. Ever since the Dutch settled and planted cabbages in America in the 1600s, there have been regional variations of coleslaw. Southerners make theirs like Bob's Barbecue of Creedmoor, North Carolina, does—creamy, sweet, and tart. Scoop some on top of your barbecue sandwich or on the side.

1 large head cabbage

4 tablespoons sweet pickle cubes

2 tablespoons sugar

1¹/₂ teaspoons salt

1¹/₂ teaspoons black pepper

1 teaspoon mustard

Mayonnaise (enough to mix)

Grate or chop cabbage. Mix with remaining ingredients, adjusting pepper and mayonnaise to taste. Refrigerate before serving.

Serves 6

Hush Puppies

Folklore has it that these crisply fried balls of cornmeal got their unusual name because they were fed to barking dogs to keep them quiet. Hush puppies are not only a favorite alongside barbecue, they're also served with fried fish. This version, which is served at Bob's Barbecue in Creedmoor, North Carolina, is especially delicious.

2 cups self-rising finely ground white cornmeal

1 cup self-rising flour

2 eggs, beaten

1/4 cup dehydrated onion flakes

1 cup buttermilk

Vegetable oil

Mix dry ingredients and eggs with buttermilk, just enough so mixture is stiff, not soupy. Drop with an ice-cream scooper into a skillet of hot oil. Fry until brown and done on the inside. Drain on paper towels and serve at once.

Serves 4

Baked Beans

Recipes for this barbecue side-dish staple also vary, but they almost always include brown sugar, onions, and green pepper. This version is courtesy of Carolina Treet Barbecue Sauce, and Rose Jones of Leland, North Carolina.

1 pound ground beef, cooked and drained

1/2 medium green pepper, chopped

1/2 cup Carolina Treet or other not-too-sweet barbecue sauce

1 medium onion, chopped

1/2 cup ketchup

1/4 cup brown sugar

31-ounce-can pork and beans

Mix all ingredients well. Bake in casserole dish at 350 degrees for 35 minutes.

Serves 8

49

NEW ORLEANS: UPTOWN FOOD DOWN SOUTH

A trip to New Orleans is nothing like a trip to the other great Southern cities. The tourists are rowdier, and Sundays don't belong to religion. What's more, you may have been born and bred in Virginia, but when it comes to New Orleans food, you might as well be from North Dakota.

For one thing, New Orleans food is fancy. When the French settled this port city in 1718, they brought their refined cooking techniques with them. That in itself colored the cuisine forever, but contributions of the Spanish, Africans, Choctaw, Cubans, Mexicans, and West Indians over the years have resulted in a complicated repertoire of foods that upstages the home-style cooking of Alabama and Tennessee.

And New Orleans teems with seafood. Though people in Gulfport, Mississippi, as well as Savannah, Charleston, and the other coastal areas are used to eating oysters and crabs on a daily basis, there are more inland Southerners whose idea of seafood is frozen, battered, deep-fried shrimp at Shoney's. Meanwhile at the market, salmon steaks and catfish fillets cost landlubbers a pretty penny.

And just when you think you've begun to understand Cajun-Creole New Orleans food , you get thrown a curve. For example, at The Commander's Palace, the famous Garden District restaurant owned by the even more famous Brennan family, traditional foods are constantly reinterpreted in the "haute Creole" mode. The classic Shrimp Creole, say the Brennans, "used to be made with a thick tomato paste, but now we use only fresh diced tomatoes. The result is not a heavy sauce, but rather a beautiful glaze." Café au lait, a rich concoction of coffee and steamed milk, is always served at breakfast and after dinner, but the Brennans have taken this institution one step further with their Café au Lait Soufflé.

On the other side of the tracks, restaurants dish out local favorites like they're going out of style—even though many of these foods have never known widespread popularity like that enjoyed by blackened redfish and jambalaya. Across the street from the French Market, in a cluttered Italian deli known as Central Grocery, people line up for mufalettas: built-for-two, olive-oily sandwiches layered with imported meat, cheese, and pickles. At outdoor jazz festivals and flea markets, vendors sell po' boys: a sandwich of French bread and fried oysters, alligator sausage, softshell crabs, or whatever goes well with a dash of Louisiana hot sauce.

Meanwhile, back at the Acme Oyster House in the French Quarter, patrons stand at a marble-topped bar, swill Dixie beer, and slurp oysters on the half shell. And just a few blocks away at Ole N'awlins Cookery, waiters with no time to spare take order upon order for barbecued shrimp and gumbo.

So even though there's always something new to try in New Orleans, the old standards continue to delight natives and tourists alike. For Southerners, New Orleans is a hot spot among an entire region of extraordinary foods. It's part of the culture, but it's anything but commonplace. In fact, one of the nicest things about having this festive city on Southern turf is that residents don't have to leave the south to sample a slice of exotica.

HOW TO EAT A CRAWFISH

They look like little lobsters, and when they're brought to the table in a steamy pile they cause quite a stir among the uninitiated. But in the Gulf Coast, crawfish (also known as crayfish, mudbugs, and crawdaddies) are a common sight in the kitchen, particularly from late winter to early summer, which is the crawfish season. The tails are apt to turn up in most any Cajun dish, but real men and women like to tackle boiled, seasoned mudbugs whole, with all their parts intact. Here's how, according to the Greater New Orleans Tourist and Convention Commission:

Grasp the head between the thumb and forefinger of one hand and the tail between the thumb and forefinger of your other hand. Slightly twist and firmly pull until the fish breaks open where the tail and body shell connect. Temporarily discard the head. Squeeze tail between thumb and forefinger until the shell cracks. Lift and loosen the three shell segments, and pull around the meat. Now take the tail fin and last shell segment between the thumb and forefinger of one hand, and the meat with the other. Gently separate the meat from the shell and pull the vein free. Discard the shell and vein and pop the meat in your mouth. What you'll get for your pains: a spicy nugget of seafood that tastes like a cross between shrimp and lobster. And when you're done with that, you can make like a native and suck the tasty juice from the crawfish head. Get cracking.

53

54

Blackened Redfish

Like so many other Louisiana specialties, blackened redfish is very popular—and very spicy! The secret is a hot, hot pan. Don't worry, though, it can't get too hot for this dish.

1 tablespoon salt

1 teaspoon onion powder

1 teaspoon cayenne pepper

1 teaspoon garlic powder

1/2 teaspoon white pepper

1/2 teaspoon dry mustard

1/2 teaspoon rubbed sage

1/2 teaspoon ground cumin

1/2 teaspoon black pepper

1/2 teaspoon dried thyme leaves

2 fresh redfish fillets

1³/₄ sticks butter, melted

Combine seasonings. Dip fish in butter, then cover each side generously and evenly with seasoning.

Heat a heavy cast-iron skillet until it is very hot and beyond the smoking stage, for at least 10 minutes.

Add seasoned fish to skillet, and cook for a minute or two, until the underside is very brown. Turn once and cook the other side.

Serves 2

Jambalaya

Each person's version of jambalaya is different. But the idea is to "sweep up the kitchen" and toss everything handy in a pot. In any case, rice, tomatoes, and lots of spices are a must.

2 tablespoons salad oil

1 onion, coarsely chopped

1 green bell pepper, coarsely chopped

3 ribs celery, coarsely chopped

5 cloves of garlic, minced

2 pounds shrimp, peeled and deveined

1/2 teaspoon thyme

2 28-ounce cans stewed tomatoes

1 cup chicken broth

1 teaspoon cayenne pepper

1/4 cup Worcestershire sauce

1/2 pound ham, cut into strips and fried

1 pound smoked sausage (Creole, andouille, or Italian), sliced and fried

3 cups raw white rice

Salt to taste

Heat oil in a large, heavy pot. Add onion, bell pepper, celery, and garlic, and sauté for 5 minutes. Add shrimp and thyme and cook over medium heat until shrimp is pink. Add tomatoes, broth, cayenne pepper, and Worcestershire, and mix well. Add sausage and ham and cook over moderate heat until mixture boils. Add rice and salt and cook over low heat until rice is tender and liquid is absorbed, about 30 minutes.

Serves 6

CAJUN COFFEE BREAK

Drinks flow freely in the city of New Orleans, especially in the bar-happy French Quarter. But when the party's over, or the dinner dishes have been cleared, or when morning breaks, as the case may be, it's time for coffee.

And such coffee! Not for the weak-kneed (on the other hand, maybe it is), New Orleans coffee is a potent mix of dark roast ground with chicory, an herbal root with a powerful flavor of its own. This special blend, which dates from the Napoleonic era, is so full-bodied that it can stand up to a generous shot of cream. The ever-popular café au lait recipe calls for equal parts of this coffee and boiling milk, whereas café noir drinkers take theirs black.

Chicory-blend coffee isn't served everywhere in the south, but you can get all you want in the French Market, where a 24-hour coffee stand has been in operation since the 1860's. This is also where you won't be able to resist an order of the deep-fried, sugar-powdered pastries they call beignets. There are many charming things to be said about taking your café au lait and beignets at the Café du Monde. But one great thing is that diners are spared the indecisiveness they experience at other restaurants—the only foods on the minimal menu are coffee, beignets, and milk.

56

FOODS

Iced Tea

No self-respecting Southern refrigerator is without a pitcher of this "sweet tea."

6 *regular-size tea bags*

1 *cup sugar*

Heat 1 quart water until the tea kettle sings. Pour over tea bags and allow to sit until tepid or cool—at least thirty minutes to an hour.

Discard tea bags and pour tea into a pitcher. Add sugar and stir until dissolved, then add another quart of water. Refrigerate.

Makes 2 quarts

Sylvia's Turnips and Collard Greens

Sylvia's restaurant, in New York City's Harlem, is a long way from Sylvia Wood's childhood home in Hemingway, South Carolina—but you wouldn't think so when you see all the transplanted Southerners lined up outside, waiting for a table. This particular version of greens, compliments of Sylvia's, is memorable.

1¹/₂ *pounds meaty ham hocks or*
ham bones

4 *cups cold water*

2¹/₂ *pounds fresh turnips, with greens*

2¹/₂ *pounds fresh collard greens*

2 *tablespoons sugar*

2 *teaspoons salt*

1¹/₂ *teaspoons black pepper*

1 *teaspoon crushed red pepper*

Place hamhocks in a very large pot. Add water and bring to a boil over medium heat. Let cook uncovered about 1 hour, until reduced to about 1 cup of broth. Remove roots from turnip greens. Wash and peel roots, cut into 1-inch slices, and add the roots to the pot. Cover and bring to a boil over medium heat, then reduce heat and allow to simmer for about ten minutes.

Remove and discard tough stems and yellowed leaves from turnip and collard greens. Wash thoroughly, drain, then chop greens into 2-inch pieces. Add to the pot. Stir in sugar, salt, and black and red pepper. Cover (you may need to weigh down the lid) and cook about 30 minutes, stirring occasionally. Reduce heat to low, and allow to simmer ten minutes or until tender.

Serves 8

Black-Bottom Pecan Pie

Georgia is the biggest pecan producer, but all of the Southern states deserve credit for the ubiquitous pecan pie. This recipe is particularly special because it incorporates the whiskey of Kentucky (or Tennessee) and the chocolate-layered crust of Mississippi.

1 *unbaked deep-dish piecrust*

1/2 *cup semisweet chocolate chips*

2 *eggs*

3/4 *cup dark corn syrup*

1/2 *cup sugar*

1/4 *teaspoon salt*

1/4 *cup butter (margarine can also be used), melted*

2 *tablespoons bourbon*

1 *cup pecan halves*

Preheat oven to 350 degrees. Sprinkle chocolate chips evenly over bottom of crust. In large bowl, beat together eggs, corn syrup, sugar, and salt with fork.

Add butter and bourbon, and beat until blended. Pour mixture in crust over chocolate chips. Arrange pecans in circles over filling.

Bake 55 minutes, or until pie tests done in the middle.

Serves 8

Cube Steak

The dish is otherwise known as country-fried steak or chicken-fried steak. Use the pan drippings to make milk gravy (see page 42) and serve it with mashed potatoes or biscuits.

2 to 3 *tablespoons vegetable oil*

4 to 5 *pieces of cube steak or tenderized round steak*

Flour (enough to coat steak)

Salt and pepper to taste

In a large nonstick skillet, heat oil to 350 degrees. Coat steak on either side with flour, and add to the skillet. Season with salt and pepper to taste. Fry for 20 or so minutes, turning once, until steak is browned and cooked through. Add oil if steaks stick.

Adjust temperature or cover skillet if steaks seem to be cooking too quickly.

Serves 4

HUNGRY FOR HOME

"Over the years, I think I've learned something about what Southern people like to eat," chef Paul Prudhomme wrote, in *Southern Magazine*, "and one thing is you can't push their tastes too far from what they're used to."

Certainly, for every Southerner who wouldn't touch baba ganoush with a ten-foot pole there's another who won't touch fried okra. Yet, once you pass the Mason-Dixon line or the Mississippi River, it's safe to say that people with highly adventurous tastes are outnumbered. The idea is that food ought to be more satisfying than surprising.

If Southerners are famous for their sedentary palates, maybe it's because they're famous for their attachment to home. It's no secret that home is never too far from a Southerner's mind, even if home wasn't a happy place. As Truman Capote once said, "All Southerners go home sooner or later, even if in a box."

Here then are some classic homestyle recipes.

Sweet Potato Casserole

At the Wood's Family Restaurant in Ridgeland, Mississippi, Dorothy M. Nichols whips up this recipe (in mega-proportions) for a buffet line that's groaning with home-style foods.

2 *pounds sweet potatoes, baked, peeled and cut up*

1/2 *cup white sugar*

2 *tablespoons brown sugar*

2 *tablespoons sweet milk*

1 *tablespoon cornstarch*

1/2 *cup raisins*

1 *egg*

1 *tablespoon margarine*

Dash vanilla extract

1/8 *teaspoon apple spice seasoning*

1/8 *teaspoon cinnamon*

1 *cup or so miniature marshmallows*

Preheat oven to 350 degrees. In the bowl of an electric mixer, add sweet potatoes. As you mix, gradually add ingredients—except for marshmallows—until they reach a creamy texture. Put into a baking pan and cook for 45 minutes. Dot top of casserole with marshmallows, and brown in oven or under broiler until light golden brown.

Serves 8

Green Beans

During the cold months, dried red beans and black-eyed peas hit the spot. But in the spring, old-fashioned cooks can hardly wait to break the season's first fresh green beans. Naturally, a chunk of fatback (the meat between the pig's skin and ribs) is required to add the "countrified" flavor of the old South.

1 pound green beans, washed, strings removed, broken into 2- to 3-inch pieces

3-inch slice of fatback, scored (bacon or a pork bone may be substituted)

Salt and pepper to taste

Put beans and fatback in a large, heavy saucepan, and add barely enough water to cover. Bring to a boil, then lower heat, cover, and simmer about an hour. Stir occasionally, making sure there's enough water to prevent beans from burning. (If water evaporates quickly, the temperature is too high.) Season with salt and pepper.

Remove cover, and allow the broth to cook down another 30 minutes, or until beans are done.

Serves 6

Mamma's Corn Bread

During antebellum days, biscuits were served on wealthy plantation tables, and the ordinary farmer ate corn bread because cornmeal was a less expensive ingredient. These days, some recipes include sugar and eggs, but a purist would tell you that those ingredients only distract from the good, honest taste of corn. (For an old-fashioned late-night snack, put leftover chunks of corn bread in a glass, pour on some cold milk, then eat it with a spoon). This recipe is from Thelma Van Deman, of Piney Flats, Tennessee.

1 tablespoon bacon grease or vegetable oil

2 cups self-rising cornmeal

2/3 cup milk

1/3 cup water

Add grease or oil to a large cast-iron skillet and preheat the skillet in a 475 degree oven. Without overmixing, stir together cornmeal, milk, and water in a bowl. When skillet is very hot, pour in cornmeal mixture.

Bake about 20 to 25 minutes, until cornbread is golden brown and done in the middle.

Serves 6

62

FOODS

Fried Chicken

It seems like everyone in Savannah has eaten their fill at Mrs. Wilkes' Boarding House, where Sema Wilkes has been serving her fried chicken since World War II. Fried chicken, of course, is a much-celebrated food all over the South.

2 *tablespoons evaporated milk*

2 *tablespoons water*

2 1/2 *pound frying chicken, cut up and sprinkled with salt and pepper to taste*

All-purpose flour (enough to coat the chicken)

Vegetable oil (enough to completely cover the chicken)

Mix milk and water and pour over chicken. Marinate about ten minutes. Dip chicken in bowl of flour and shake off excess.

Deep-fry chicken when oil reaches 300 degrees. Make sure chicken is covered with oil at all times. Fry until golden brown. (This recipe may also be used to fry pork chops.)

Serves 4

Fried Catfish

In places like Belzoni, Mississippi, and Toad Suck, Arkansas, catfish is the cat's meow. Though there are quite a few towns that call themselves "the catfish capital of the world," most Southerners can appreciate this distinctly Dixie-ish fish.

4 *single-serving-sized catfish, cleaned and skinned*

Salt to taste

Cornmeal (enough to coat)

Solid vegetable shortening

Black pepper to taste

Sprinkle fish with salt and dip in cornmeal. In a large iron skillet, melt shortening to about 1 inch in depth. Heat to about 375 degrees, or until the pan is quite hot but not smoking.

Carefully lay fish in the skillet without crowding. Fry 3 to 4 minutes on each side, or until golden brown, turning the fish only once.

Drain on paper towels and add pepper.

Serves 4

Tennessee Blackberry Wine Cake

Unlike many other recipes, blackberry wine cake isn't found in every Southern cookbook. Yet, it deserves inclusion here for two reasons. For one, blackberries grow wild in the south and, in the summer, often find their way into pies and cobblers. So we've grown fond of the taste. For another, Shannon Sitton, who now lives in Norfolk, Virginia, and who grew up in Signal Mountain, Tennessee, says her aunt makes this cake every Christmas and it's misery just waiting 364 days a year to taste it. And if that ain't good home cooking, what else is?

1 box Duncan Hines white cake mix

3-ounce box blackberry Jello

2 eggs

1/2 cup oil

3/4 cup blackberry wine

Preheat oven to 350 degrees. In large bowl, combine cake mix and Jello until well blended. Add eggs, oil, and wine. With an electric mixer, mix at low speed for 2 minutes—no more, no less.

Pour batter in greased bundt cake pan. Bake 30 to 40 minutes, until cake tests done.

Makes one cake

Dorothy Hopkins' Peach Cobbler

Ask Gwen Hopkins, who lives in Nashville, what she remembers best about her childhood home in Cairo, Georgia, and she'll rattle off a half dozen of her mom's desserts. Naturally, many of them feature Georgia's beloved peaches.

1¹/2 cups fresh peaches

1 cup sugar

1/4 pound margarine (1 stick)

1 cup all-purpose flour

1 to 2 drops vanilla extract

1/2 cup milk

Preheat oven to 375 degrees. Cover fruit with 1/2 cup sugar and let stand. Melt margarine in a 10- by 13-inch baking dish.

Meanwhile, mix together flour, remaining 1/2 cup sugar, vanilla, and milk to make pourable batter. Add peaches to baking dish, pour batter mixture on top, and bake about 40 minutes, or until done.

Serves 8

65

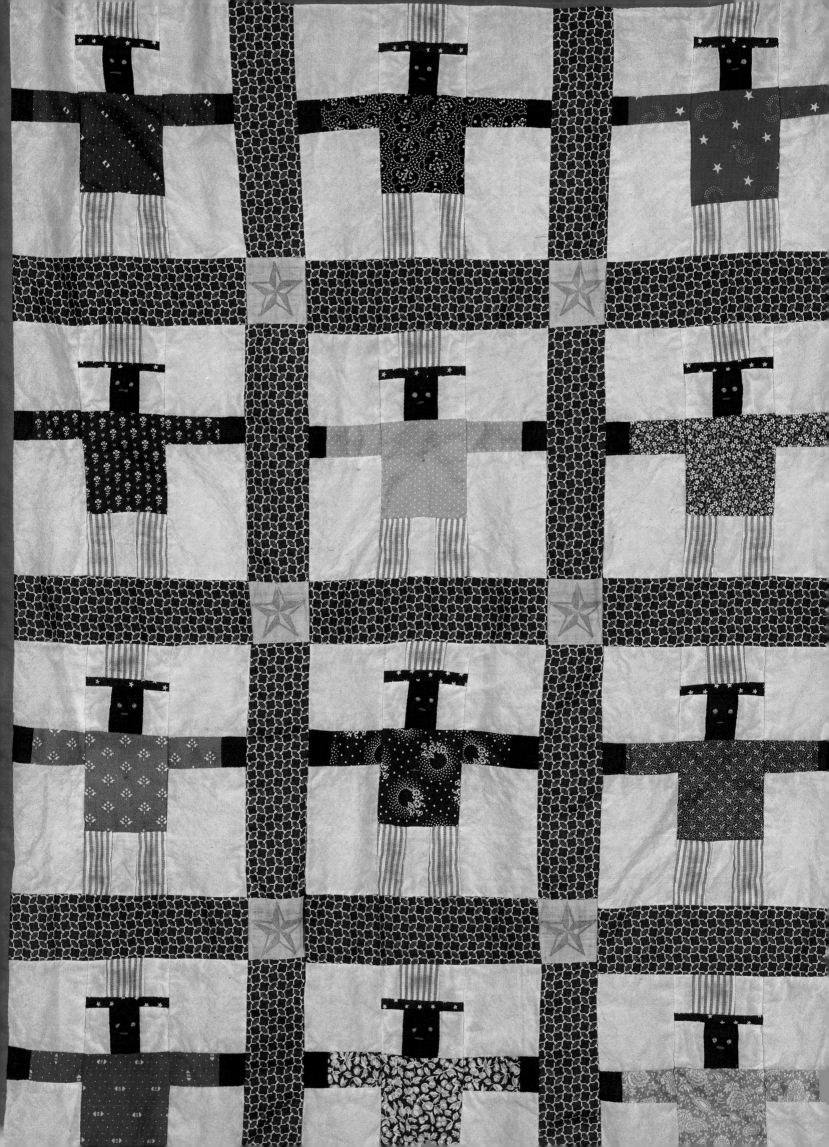

SOUTHERN CRAFTS & COLLECTIBLES

It's impossible to write about crafts without writing about the people who make them. A walking cane made by Papaw *(that's grandfather to you non-Southerners) is more cherishable than a walking cane made by a stranger. And in this book, it's the craftspeople who make the crafts come to life. (Fortunately, they're willing to share their secrets.)*

Most of the folk arts that we classify as Southern could be put in the larger category of Early American folk arts. But Southerners don't usually lump their quilts in the same category as the quilts of New England. And while pottery may have roots that extend as far west as Colorado, the people of North Carolina and Georgia have a colorful history of pottery making all their own.

Of course, part of what makes a craft Southern is the use of indigenous materials. Naturally, our ancestors reached for the materials native to the land in order to create the things they needed—brooms, cookware, baskets, bed covers, even musical instruments and toys. And broomcorn was easily grown in the warm Southern climate, so that's what some people used to make brooms. Other materials were also used, depending on the region. Mississippians used sedge; people in coastal areas crafted with palmetto; and mountain dwellers of North Carolina typically used buckeye. When old-time Southerners needed a basket for hauling cotton or carrying lunch, they chopped down the oak trees that grew nearby, or gathered the pine needles or sweet grass that crossed their paths.

Southerners can't take credit for all hand-crafted toys, but they can stake a claim to the dugout boats made from cypress driftwood and the palmetto doll dresses of Louisiana. Even when Southerners make a craft that's similar to those made in other parts of the country, there's usually something distinctively regional about it. For example, you can tell that a hardwood slat-back chair is definitely Southern when its rear posts are curved backward and front surfaces are shaved back.

68

*T*he Uncle Sam quilt (page 66), is a contemporary pattern, made in 1986 by Stephen Blumrich, who runs a small quilt shop in Tullahoma, Tennessee. Broom and basket weaving (this page) are part of the rich tradition of Southern crafts.

MAKING BROOMS, MAKING FRIENDS

*B*rooms are a traditional Southern craft, born of necessity, much like baskets and pottery. The utilitarian nature of hand made brooms is overshadowed by their beauty.

There was Mattie Pearl, who might have been any full-figured, gray-haired woman except for her eyes—so dark and warm they melted formality—and her voice—pleasantly low-pitched and confident with country know-how. And there was Gladys, a friend of Mattie Pearl's, similar in age and experience but with a childlike timidity. Nathan was the only man, and Jackie was the prettiest, whereas Betty was a big talker, and Violet never said a word. And Hazel, a raspy-voiced, sixty-eight-year-old mountain woman who dressed in workshirts and caps, was our teacher. It was spring in Montreat, North Carolina, and we were learning to make brooms.

Make brooms? For all the under-sixty set knows, brooms are born and raised at department stores. But today's factory-spawned tool is a descendant of a sturdier, more handsome broom that dates back to the 1780s, when the broomcorn plant was first transplanted from India. At that time, Southerners took to planting a few rows of the sorghumlike broomcorn with their annual crop of corn. The practice of using handmade brooms gradually diminished by the mid-fifties, as mass-produced versions made from imported, processed broomcorn or synthetics became common.

These days, craftspeople are concerned that broom making, like many forms of folk life, will be forgotten. But people like Mattie Pearl, Gladys, and the other members of the North Carolina Agricultural Extension Service are helping to see that the craft stays alive.

At our first broom-making session, we bypassed a lot of the initial, time-consuming aspects of the craft. Hazel explained, "I have got a lot of the work already done for you," as she passed out presorted bundles of broom and hardwood sticks that would serve as handles. The "corn" came from her garden in Horse Shoe, the alder from a creek bank near her property. Hazel described her four-foot rows of corn, while Mattie Pearl showed the others how honeysuckle vines had reshaped the wood handles.

When Hazel dropped an assortment of cord on the table, Nathan chose basic black. Betty exclaimed, "Isn't the green gorgeous?" but settled on black as well, while Violet silently selected a mauve cord. Meanwhile, Hazel explained how her "grandpap" taught her to lace brooms with strings made from grounding skins or sometimes from hay-baling wires.

We used currycombs to remove seeds that clung to "the sweep" (Mattie Pearl saved hers to plant later) and then employed sharp knives to slice off half the stems. The bundles of stalks were wrapped in towels, and stem ends were soaked in buckets of hot water while the class went to lunch.

Later, the broom makers retrieved their bundles and lined up the stalks in

CRAFTS AND COLLECTIBLES

SOUTHERN SEMANTICS

When Hazel the broom-making teacher cracked, "I may not have a long pedigree but I bet I'd get out of the rain faster than you," what she meant was, "I may not have a lot of education, but I've got more common sense than you."

The fact that our elders prefer common sense (knowing how to pick a trustworthy person as well as a ripe tomato) to "book learning" is a recurring theme in Southern culture. Although "pedigree" in this context doesn't crop up often in today's language, the colorful expressions of our ancestors do. Hazel's comment is a play off the well-known phrase, "He doesn't have enough sense to come in out of the rain."

We don't give our language much thought until we find ourselves in the company of amused non-Southerners. But every once in a while, somebody will let fly with an expression that leaves everyone in the room laughing, Southerners and all. Here are some of our favorites:

Well if that don't beat the hen pecking with a wooden bill.

She was broad as a barn.

He was as nervous as a long-tailed cat in a room full of rocking chairs.

His teeth were so crooked he could eat corn on the cob through a picket fence.

He's lying like a rug.

He's as ugly as a mud fence.

He was running around like a chicken with his head cut off.

He's as naked as a jaybird.

She was as mad as a wet hen.

size from smallest to largest. When the stalks were eventually wrapped around the stick, the small stalks would be on the inside while the larger ones would fill out the outside.

Then Hazel handed out what she called "sack needles"—heavy and 6 inches long, they reminded the older women of the needles once used to sew up mattresses. The water had softened the stem ends so it was possible to push the needle through and string the stalks together. So after measuring out a yard (almost a meter) of cord at a time (Mattie Pearl did it the old-fashioned way, by holding one end in her outstretched right hand, turning her head to the left, and stretching the cord to her nose), the class set about their handiwork.

For two days, the broom makers weaved their needles in and out of their bundles with the most intimidating amount of ease—none of them were strangers to craft work. Meanwhile, Hazel made wisecracks ("Honey, I may not have a long pedigree, but I bet I'd get out of the rain faster than you"); Jackie said it was a shame that young people didn't take an interest in old crafts; and Gladys fretted because she didn't think her stitches were straight enough.

Come to find out that Gladys' rust-stitched broom was one of the prettiest, although everyone had cause to be proud. Perhaps the proudest of all was Hazel, who first lined up the brooms, then the class members, for Polaroids. But the ultimate compliment came when Hazel picked up a broom—it didn't matter whose—and started in on the broomcorn seeds littering the floor. She looked up and a bodacious grin crossed her face. "I'll have you to know this broom will sweep sugar."

*T*oday, an old-fashioned handmade broom is more likely to be decorative than functional. But before there were manufactured brooms, vacuum cleaners, and carpet sweepers, homemade brooms were essential housekeeping tools.

73

CRAFTS AND COLLECTIBLES

HOW TO MAKE A BROOM

Materials Needed

Broomcorn: It's best if you raise broomcorn or if you know someone who does. This way, the corn is inexpensive, handy, and available in small amounts instead of in bulk. You'll want corn that was harvested in mid-July and dried for at least two weeks. Select a bundle with a uniform sweep and 6- to 8-inch stems—how much depends on the size of your corn and broom. About 25 stalks were used in the hearth broom directions that follow. If the corn is very large, it may be desirable to cut the stem ends in half.

Knife: A small sharp one, such as a paring knife, is ideal for cutting broomcorn.

Towel: An old one for wrapping up broomcorn is needed. It may be desirable to protect your clothes with another old towel, or else wear an apron.

Bucket: This is needed for soaking the broomcorn stems.

Wood: For the hearthbroom directions below, select a stick about 2 feet long and about 1 inch in diameter or 3/4 inch square. Hardwood such as alder or maple is ideal—especially if it's been twisted by vines or has some other interesting character. But it's also possible to use a round extra-large dowel or an old sanded-down broom handle. Whisk brooms, of course, require no handle at all, whereas housecleaning brooms require long handles.

Nails: Two short finishing nails or tacks for securing the sweep are necessary.

Hammer: Use this for hammering down sharp ends and creating a flat broom.

Cord: About 6 yards of strong thread—colored cotton cord, nylon cord, or no. 7- to 10-gauge linen cord will do. These materials are available in shops that carry macrame supplies.

Needle: A heavy, 6-inch bagging or needlepoint needle is required. Look in needlepoint shops, or contact an upholsterer.

Beeswax: This is available at quilt shops, boot factories, or from beekeepers.

Gloves: To protect your hands as you stitch, wear gardening gloves or any cotton gloves.

75

CRAFTS AND COLLECTIBLES

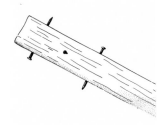

4

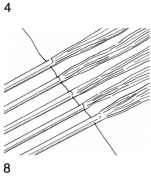

8

12

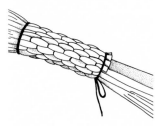

14

17

Directions

1. Remove seeds from broomcorn with comb or fork.

2. Lay out the stalks of broomcorn on a table with the stem ends closest to you. Place a knife about 1½ inches below where the stem begins and the brush ends. Begin to cut at an angle, then continue to slice off half the stem all the way to its end. Do this with all stalks.

3. Wrap broomcorn in towel and soak the stems, not the brush, in a bucket of hot water for at least 30 minutes.

4. While stems soak, prepare handle. Into one side, drive one nail 1½ inches from the top of the handle. Into the other side, drive the second nail 3 inches from the top. Both nails should project about ⅛ inch on each side of the wood. This will keep the brush from slipping. (If desired, drill a hole in the end of the handle for hanging up later as a decorative element.)

5. Remove the stems from the water. Line them up on the table from largest on the left to smallest on the right, with the sliced stems face up and closest to you.

6. Measure about 6 yards of cord and tie a knot about 2 inches from the end. Thread the other end through the needle.

7. Run the needle and cord through the beeswax a few times.

8. Put on gloves. Beginning with the smallest stems, string broomcorn together with needle and cord. To do this, run the needle through the sides of the uncut 1½-inch part of the stem, making sure the sliced part of the stem is still face up. As you go, push broomcorn as close as possible to the knotted end of the cord.

9. Attach the knotted end of the cord to one of the handle's nails by tying a slipknot.

10. Roll the brush around the handle carefully so the nails pierce and secure the stems. Make sure the handle is in the center of the broom. Tie string around the sweep of the broom to protect it.

11. After the corn is around the handle, step on the loose cord so it's taut. Then turn the broom in your hands so the cord winds around tightly 3 times. Cracking or popping noises are normal.

12. Fasten securely with evenly placed whipstitches around and over these cords. Depending on the size of your broomcorn, a stitch every 3 stems is about right.

13. On the last whipstitch, push the needle up, pull the cord through, and begin weaving. Take the needle and cord over a stem, then under the next, over the next, and so on. Continue to weave around and around the top of the broom. Make sure the stitches alternate, and push the stitches as close, tight, and straight as possible.

14. Weave up the handle 4 to 5 inches. Then tightly wind the cord around the handle 2 times. Fasten securely with evenly placed whipstitches—the same as in step 12.

15. Use knife to trim uneven stems about 1 inch from the cord.

16. On the last whipstitch, work the needle and cord down through the handle to about 1 or 2 inches below the first whipstitches from step 12. (Push the needle behind the stems so the cord does not show.)

17. Again, wrap the cord around the broom 3 times and secure with whipstitches. Move down a few more inches, wrap, and whipstitch. Move down another few inches, wrap, and stitch. (If a flat broom with a wide sweep is desired, use the hammer to pound the heavy shank of the broom before winding and whipstitching. Then place two 2- to 3-inch wide boards on top and beneath the lower part of the sweep; tie flat with strings on the ends. Then wrap and whipstitch as explained here.)

18. Use the knife to trim uneven stems about 1 inch from the top row of cord and whipstitches. Then use knife to shape the bottom of the sweep.

19. Use hammer to gently pound the handle to ensure nails aren't piercing through.

20. If desired, crochet a string or tie a buckskin string in order to hang broom for display.

©Lynn Karlin

77

BASKETS

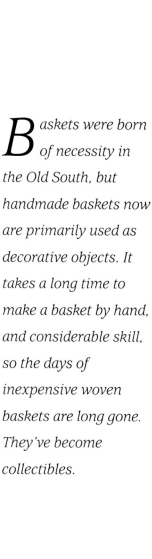

Baskets were born of necessity in the Old South, but handmade baskets now are primarily used as decorative objects. It takes a long time to make a basket by hand, and considerable skill, so the days of inexpensive woven baskets are long gone. They've become collectibles.

Whatever happened to the days when handmade baskets held everything from babies to tobacco, from fish to feathers? Native Americans even fashioned baskets that carried water, whereas pioneers developed the one-sided egg basket, ideal for hanging on the wall and attaching to a horse saddle.

Like so many handmade goods, baskets created out of necessity were gradually replaced by manufactured items—paper bags, plastic buckets, glass jars—after the turn of the century. (Factory-made versions have never been as strong as handmade baskets.) But for years now, various factions in the South have sought to keep this Early American craft alive. In the twenties and thirties, New Deal agencies and craft guilds first appeared on the scene with an interest in documenting Southern work. In the forties, the Bureau of Indian Affairs introduced basket-making and basket-marketing programs, designed to increase the income of Native American communities. And from the sixties to the present, an interest in history, cultural preservation, and crafts has kept basket making alive.

These very same influences have changed the nature of modern-day basket making, too. Baskets that were once made to be purses or to hold peaches are now filled with potpourri or plants. Meanwhile, many of the people who make them today aren't motivated by the need for a new cotton basket or lunch basket, but by a desire to make additional income or simply to create a handmade object. Yet, many basketmakers are like R.L. McGaha, of Franklin, North Carolina, who recently took it up as a hobby.

©William Seitz

CRAFTS AND COLLECTIBLES

There are three major traditions of Southern basket-making: Native American, African American and Anglo-American. Distinctive characteristics remain in each group. For example, Native Americans favor split reed, willow, and grasses, as do craftsmen. Anglo-Americans and African Americans prefer white oak, hickory, and other hardwood stock.

© Christopher Bain

Ironically, his schedule is similar to that of the first American settlers: In the daytime, he's chopping wood or feeding cattle. When he's "sitting around at night," especially winter nights, he might work on a basket for an hour or two. "One winter I made eighteen," says McGaha, who's sixty-nine and "proud of every year." He's slacked off, though, since he only sold two, and the rest he gave away. "I didn't plan on making much but I thought I might make a little." Apparently, fifty dollars or so was a price many customers weren't willing to pay, though it's reasonable when you consider the cost of the reed (about ten dollars per basket) and the time (about twelve hours for one well-made, "not thrown together," egg basket).

Yet, the man isn't exactly lacking an appreciative audience. He tells the story of two women who looked at his work, then instead of buying, signed up for a basket-making class. "They come back saying, 'Lord 'a' mercy! Those baskets take a lot of work!'" McGaha doesn't smile or chuckle, but his eyes are enjoying a good laugh.

BASKET ROUNDUP

Split-oak: Basket weavers like R.L. McGaha use a commercial reed that's sold in hobby shops, but a few craftspeople still split their own wood. Ash, hickory, buckeye, or palmetto make sturdy materials, but in Kentucky, Tennessee, and North Carolina, white oak is plentiful and ideal for baskets.

According to Gregg Gulley of Dollywood, the cutting process requires about eight hours—from the first axcrack of a sapling, 8 inches in diameter, to the last pocketknife-peel of a split, $^1/_{16}$ of an inch. The splits are then soaked to make them pliable and woven into any one of several shapes, from the small "hip" basket, formed by a deeply indented center rib into two sections, to a large cotton basket, wide-mouthed and at one time designed to carry up to one hundred (100) pounds of cotton.

Honeysuckle: Although not as strong as split-oak baskets, honeysuckle, river willow, and grapevine are other popular basket materials throughout the South. Gathered when the sap is down, honeysuckle vines are boiled for four hours before the bark is peeled away. After they have been soaked in cold water, hung in the sun to dry, and stripped of small knots with a knife, weaving begins. Some artisans, such as Joyce Taylor of the Eastern Band of Cherokee, bleach the vines or use natural dyes (walnut, and bloodroot, for instance) to color the vines prior to weaving.

River cane: "This plant," says Jan Arnow, the author of By Southern Hands, *"has played a vital role in dozens of Native American cultures, from the Cherokees in the Great Smoky Mountains to the Chitimachas along the coast of southern Louisiana." The cane is gathered from swampy areas—about fifty sticks are used per basket—dyed in walnut hulls or roots, then woven into the geometric designs so characteristic of the Native Americans. According to Arnow, double-walled river-cane baskets can hold water, since cane swells when it gets wet.*

Palmetto: The palmetto may be South Carolina's state tree, but Louisiana is best known for its palmetto baskets and wide-brimmed hats. The circular-shaped fronds are harvested from marshy areas, slit into $^1/_4$ inch strands, and allowed to sun-dry for several weeks. The strands are then plaited, coiled, and sewn together with brightly colored thread.

Pine needle: The Southern pine, with needles that measure from 12 to 18 inches, aren't plentiful where Stella Martin lives in Johnson City, Tennessee. But when she goes to Florida for the winter, she gathers and dries the needles to make the baskets that are native to the coasts below southern Virginia and in the Deep South. She wraps a bundle of soaked-and-dried needles in raffia and coils them in a tight spiral. Then each row lays along the edge of the preceding row, and so on. As a final charming touch, Martin tops her round sewing baskets with two tiny pinecones.

Sweet grass: Palmetto, pine needles, bulrush, and sweet grass are all used to make the African-influenced baskets of South Carolina's coastal region. Like pine-needle baskets, sweet grass baskets begin with a coil of pine needles. As the diameter expands, strands of sweet grass or rush are gradually added. Row after row is bound with a strip of palmetto frond. The result is an intricate tapestry of the native plants.

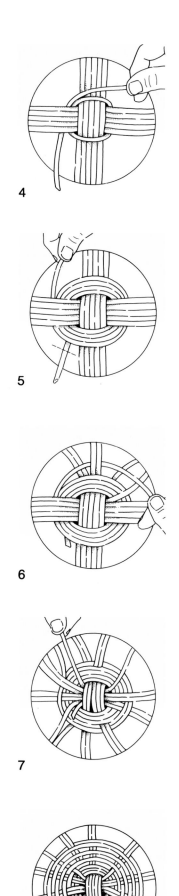

4

5

6

7

8

HOW TO MAKE A BASIC BASKET

Because natural materials aren't always available, the following directions are for a basket made from commercial reed. However, you may substitute flexible branches of willow or else weave in the soaked stems of dried flowers for a more natural look.

Materials Needed

Rattan: Obtain a 1-pound bag from a hobby shop, or use a large quantity of long split reeds.
Bucket: You will need this for soaking branches in water.

String: About 2 or 3 feet or opt for raffia, the fiber of the raffia palm used for making crafts and tying plants: It's ideal for tying short reeds together to lengthen them.

Directions

1. Choose 10 long reed or willow strands to make the "spokes" of the basket.

2. Soak all the strands in water for 1 hour.

3. On a table, lay 5 long strands across the other 5 long strands so they form a cross.

4. Take another strand, and slide it under one group of 5 long spokes. Weave it over the

7. Select an unused strand. Push one end of this strand through a hole at the base of the weaving, then bring the other end back up after passing it under a few strands. Trim the short end of this strand so it doesn't stick out—the idea is to use the long end as a new spoke. An even number of spokes (the new ones you created by separating the original spokes into pairs) causes you to weave over and under the same spokes each time, whereas this additional, odd spoke allows you to alternate weaving.

8. Continue to weave under and over the paired-off strands, treating the new single spoke as a pair. Weave flat until the base is big enough to accommodate your size basket.

9. Weave one more round, separating the pairs of spokes and weaving under and over each individual strand.

10. Turn the strands up in the direction that you'll weave the basket walls and loosely tie the strands with string.

11. Continue to weave between the individual strands. When the basket wall is strong enough to stand on its own, remove the string.

12. When the basket reaches the desired height, be sure to leave at least 4 inches of protruding spokes on top. One by one, bend these strands down and weave them in and out, down through the basket wall, until they are secure.

Note: If reeds or willow are too short to work with, tie several together with raffia to make long strands. At any point when you run out of a strand, add a new one by overlapping the old one. Hold it as you weave. Then, when the new strand is secure, trim the ends so that they are hidden behind a spoke.

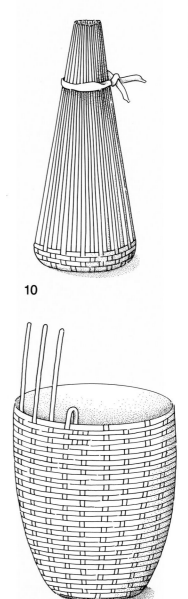

10

12

83

next 5 spokes, under the next 5, and over the next 5. Continue to weave around the spokes like this until you complete four rounds.

5. Trim the end of the strand at the point where you first began weaving. The strand is now secure and won't unravel.

6. Go back to the long end of the strand, at the point where you have just completed four rounds. Separating the spokes into pairs of strands, weave over the next 2 strands. Then weave under the next 2 strands. Then weave over the next 2 strands (these 2 strands will come from 2 different original spokes). Continue to weave under and over the pairs of strands until you've gone all the way around once.

QUILT STORIES

Quilting skills and a variety of patchwork patterns were brought to the Southern United States through the migration of settlers. A typical Anglo-American pattern is the Double Wedding Ring (right), a complex pattern that requires precise piecing.

The woman chose her steps carefully from her house to the roadside, folding her arms against the mountain chill. She presumed I was there to inquire about the quilts, and I was—but not to buy. On my many trips across the hills that separate my mother and I, it was impossible to miss that clothesline, which not only faced the curve of the highway, but also advertised a new row of quilts. In fact, I had stopped here before with friends to admire the bright colors and consider purchasing a quilt.

But this time I had something special to ask. In spite of the informal display, humble house, and Flag Pond, Tennessee, address, it was clear that this was no country-bumpkin operation. The youngish man who had tried to sell these quilts to my friends before had been quick to point out how many hours it took for a group of women to create each quilt. This was why he wouldn't take a penny less than the asked-for price. He didn't smile, either. When my friends didn't make up their minds fast enough, he left. So much for Southern hospitality, my guests from New York said, but I figure that mountain people are a special breed—they like to keep to themselves. What's more, I figure that they were doing so well (why, the quilts were replaced every time I passed) they didn't need to mince words.

So I wasn't surprised when, after the woman had picked her way across the soggy yard, her tentative smile faded. "Hi, how're you?" I ventured in my mother's twang. Then I told her how much I admired the quilts and how I would like to interview the people behind them. I started to explain about my book—but I was already losing her.

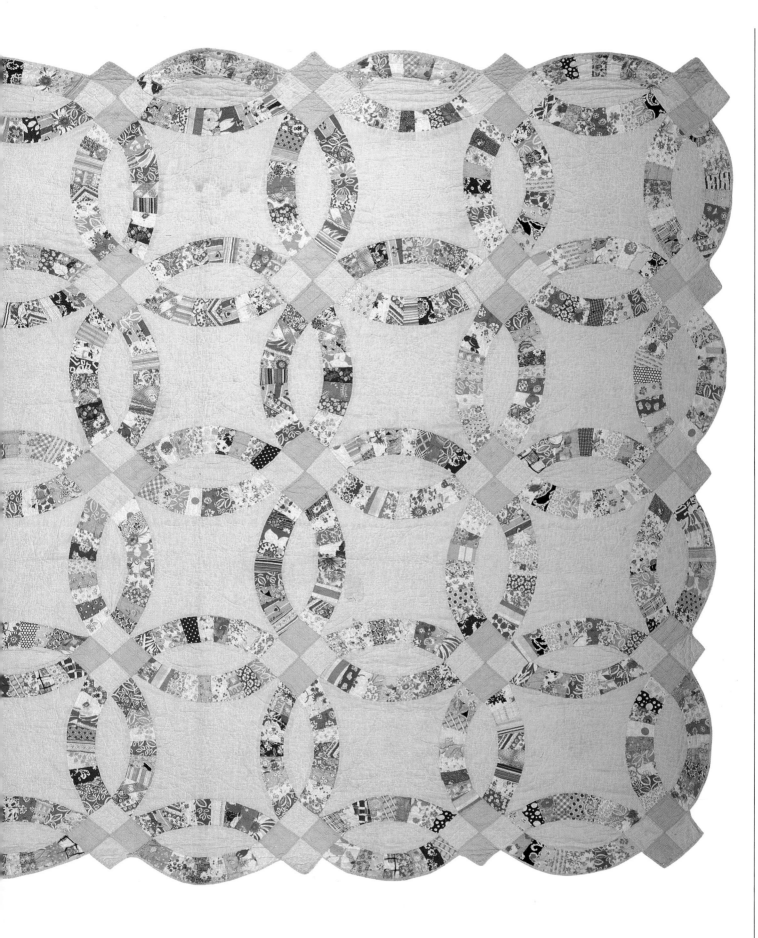

At the word "interview," she jerked her head away and gave the road a good, hard stare. Her squared shoulders hunched up another inch toward her ears. And the instant I paused, she was ready to jump in with, "I don't believe I'm interested."

Back and forth we went, me with my "trust me, trust me" advances, her with her "I done made my mind up" retreats. She seemed to soften a little when I mentioned my roots—as many times as I possibly could. I also managed to work my mother in a few times—since she seemed to be about my mother's age, I thought The Ever-Devoted Daughter Image couldn't hurt.

But finally, I gave up, thrust out my hand, and said, "Well, I've enjoyed talking to you, and I appreciate your time." You've never seen such a transition in a person. With a grin that completely changed the shape of her face, she finally uncrossed her arms and stuck out her own hand. "No hard feelings!" she said before turning up the hill.

In both of them were the scraps of dresses Grandma Dee had worn fifty and more years ago. Bits and pieces of Grandpa Jarrell's Paisley shirts. And one teeny faded blue piece, about the size of a penny matchbox, that was from Great Grandpa Ezra's uniform that he wore in the Civil War.
—Alice Walker,
"Everyday Use,"
In Love and Trouble

TAKE CARE

A quilt collection—whether it consists of family heirlooms or store-bought prizes—requires tender loving care. The following are suggestions for how to keep your quilts in optimal condition:

Storage: Roll the quilt in a bed sheet rather than folding it. Avoid plastic bags, since they keep the quilt from "breathing."

Display: The bed is as good a place as any, although some people prefer to hang their quilts on a rack or the wall. To hang a quilt, attach Velcro to the wall and baste it at corresponding locations on the quilt. It's also possible to baste loops on the quilt and hang it from a dowel that rests on nails. Quilt-hanging devices are available, too, but both of these latter two methods could possibly stress the fabric.

Light: All forms of light, particularly sunlight and fluorescent light, are potentially damaging to textiles. However, it's not always convenient or desirable to hide quilts away in a dark room. The best advice, then, is to limit direct exposure as much as possible.

Climate: Extremes of any kind—humidity, dry air, high or low temperatures—are to be avoided. Fluctuations in the climate and temperature, for example, are also undesirable.

Cleaning: Ideally, all materials should be prewashed before the quilt is constructed. Otherwise, dark colors might bleed. If you think the quilt is reasonably safe to wash, use a mild detergent on the gentle cycle. Color-fast quilts are OK to wash on warm, otherwise, go with cold or luke-warm. To air-dry, hang it out with the weight evenly distributed and clothespins along the top edge. To machine-dry, tumble on a gentle cycle.

If the condition and colorfastness of your quilt is questionable, dry-cleaning is a possibility. But talk to your dry cleaner first; there may be limitations. An extremely fragile quilt may be vacuumed; lay the quilt on a clean table, cover it with fiberglass screening, and use a low suction, hand-held vacuum with a small brush attachment.

88

*A*s in the past, quilts are still made as heirlooms or gifts to mark weddings, baby showers, and other occasions, Patterns from left to right: Sunbonnet Sue, Star, and Grape Basket.

HOW TO MAKE A PATCHWORK QUILT PLACEMAT

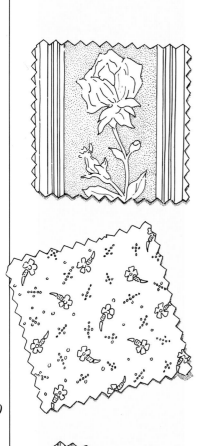

Unless you're already accomplished in needlework, it's best to begin with something small and simple. Though "quilt" is often associated with the bed covering, quilters use the word for the stitching design that goes through the pieced top, the batting in the middle, and the lining on the bottom. A patchwork quilt has a top consisting of small pieces of fabric combined into a large block shape.

Materials Needed

Pattern paper: This is available in needlework shops.

Wax pencil or felt marker: You will need this to write on pattern paper.

Ruler: This is needed to measure patchwork boxes.

Scissors: Your scissors must be sharp enough to accurately cut fabric and pattern paper.

Fabric for patchwork top, padding, and lining: For the patchwork, you can use scraps from other projects and good pieces from old clothes. But the beginner or the person who has a color scheme in mind may wish to buy new fabric. Look for a mix of print and solid cottons and cotton blends at remnant counters and discount shops. For each placement, 1 yard of polyester fleece is required for the padding. Also choose 1 yard of 45-inch wide cotton (in a color that will complement your patchwork) for each placemat. Wash all fabrics and iron before cutting.

Pencil: A fine hard lead one is essential for marking fabric and is available in art-supply or stationery stores.

Needle and thread: It's possible to use a sewing machine, but for the beginner or for small, irregularly shaped patchwork, a needle and thread are ideal.

Directions

1. Cut a 12- by 18-inch piece of pattern paper. With pencil or marker and ruler, divide the paper into 6 large rectangles. Within each of the 6 rectangles, break up the space into smaller rectangles of different sizes. Number each small shape.

2. Cut another 12- by 18-inch piece of paper. Now trace the pattern you've just made to use as a guide.

3. Cut the original pattern into individual pieces. (If you plan to make several placemats, you may wish to make a template with sandpaper and carbon paper. A template is a copy of the pattern pieces that stands up better to wear and tear of cutting fabric. Also, sandpaper has the added advantage of not slipping when it's placed on the fabric for cutting.)

4. After you decide where each fabric goes in the patchwork design, lay the first piece of fabric face down on a table. Find the straight grain of the fabric (by looking at the selvage or by pulling a thread). Place the pattern piece or template on the straight grain of the fabric; all edges should be on the lengthwise or crosswise grain.

5. With the pencil, trace the shape of the pattern on the fabric. If you'll be making more than one placemat, retrace the shape the appropriate number of times. Be sure to allow 1/4 inch (.6 centimeter) of additional fabric on each edge for cutting and, later, for seams—the pencil line represents the line for sewing, not cutting. If you'll be using this fabric for another rectangle, continue to place and trace pattern pieces. Get the most out of your fabric by placing pattern pieces carefully.

90

6. Cut each rectangle individually, making sure to allow an extra $1/4$ inch on each side of the pencil line. Be sure to keep pattern pieces organized with fabrics for easy handling.

7. Repeat steps 5 and 6 until you have the cutout pieces ready.

8. To assemble the patchwork top, begin with the pieces for one of the 6 large blocks. Refer to your guide from step 2. Firmly hold 2 small pieces together, face to face, and sew tiny running stitches along the penciled line. To fasten seams at both ends, make several back-stitches. Iron the seam open, then sew another small piece. (It may be necessary to trim excess fabric where seams cross—but with small, careful clips.)

9. Continue to sew small pieces until you have one large block. Set aside and begin another. When all the large blocks are completed for one placemat, join together in the same way.

10. Cut a 12- by 18-inch piece of the cotton lining fabric and polyester fleece padding.

11. With the cotton lining and patchwork top facing each other, and the polyester padding on top of the cotton lining, stitch the right sides together in a $1/4$-inch seam. Stitch all the way around, leaving a few inches open on one side for turning.

12. Trim the corners of excess fabric and turn it right side out. Iron, then slip-stitch the opening.

13. Finally, to quilt the fabric, use tiny, even stitches to outline each patch about $1/8$ inch on either side of the seams. Start by pushing thread up from the back, leaving a small tail of thread. Make a half-size stitch through the three layers and cover this with a second regular-size stitch. Finish the thread this same way.

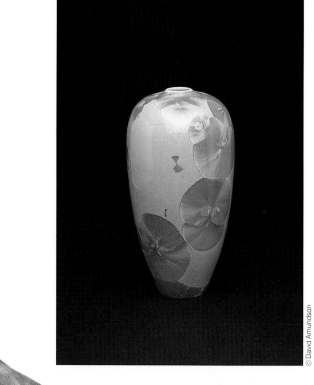

POTTERY

Before inexpensive glass, metal, and plastic containers were plentiful in America, pottery was used to store, process, and handle food and drink. Earthenware and stoneware were even more indispensable in the South, where the warm climate made food preservation a challenge.

Consequently, the craft had pockets of creators in most Southern states. Yet North Carolina—with a nod to Georgia and the Southwestern state of Texas—has always had one of the strongest pottery cultures in the South. For one reason, sedimentary clay is readily available in the soils of this state. For another, the Moravians settled in Winston-Salem in the 1700s, and since then, their highly respected crafts skills have embroidered North Carolina's cultural history.

It seems fitting, then, to visit North Carolina for a lesson in pottery making —specifically, to Creedmoor, where the

© Glenn Tucker

93

Cedar Creek Gallery has been "turning and burning" since 1969. More than twenty years ago, Sid and Pat Oakley bought ten acres and set up a little shop in this small town outside Durham. Since then, Cedar Creek Gallery has grown into the largest selection of quality crafts—not just functional stoneware, but also quilts, musical instruments, weaving, blown glass, furniture, and candles—in the southeastern United States.

You're likely to meet Sid himself when you walk in the door of this sprawling yet intimate place. His light hair is set off by old-fashioned, black-framed eyeglasses that were chosen for their modern-day funkiness or because he's never changed them.

Either way, his plain-folk friendliness belies his status among craftspeople: In 1981, a limited edition of two hundred pieces was chosen for sale in the Smithsonian Institution Catalog. In

©David Amundson

1982, President Reagan gave one of Sid Oakley's pots to the president of the Republic of Korea during an official visit. In 1988, his work was presented to Japan's ambassador to America. And the list of honors goes on and on.

But Sid won't tell you about his honors or how he makes his breathtaking, icy-pastel crystalline-glaze pots —that would not only be a breach of his modesty, it's sort of farfetched for the person who's here for the fundamentals. Instead, he directs you to where one of the resident potters is giving a demonstration.

Outside of the gallery, across the gravel parking lot, and behind some trees is the studio where Brad Tucker works. He leans forward on a straight-back chair behind his potter's wheel, surrounded by clay-splattered equipment and shelf after shelf of stoneware, fresh from the wheel and waiting for the next step.

The wheel whirls and the potter throws a chunk of clay in the center. He dips his fingers in water, and with the most fluid of motions, pushes the clay down, out, and up. His movements are *so* subtle, the clay seems to rise and fall on its own, when actually, the evolving pitcher is the product of a deft thumb here, a supporting hand there. After he has wetted his fingers a few more times and trimmed the top with a ribbed piece of steel, the wheel stops. The potter uses his thumb and finger to shape a spout for the pitcher, then separates the pitcher from the wheel with a piece of string. Later, he'll shape and attach a handle.

The potter continues to stop and start the wheel, each time giving birth to something new—a bowl, a vase, a mug. When the pots are dry, they'll be ready for their first trip to the kiln.

There are five kilns at Cedar Creek— one outside Tucker's garage-like studio, the other four a stone's throw from the

94

O pposite page:
Sid Oakley
throws a pot in his
studio. This page: a pot
created by Brad Tucker.

POTTERY, STEP BY STEP

When you're throwing a pot on the wheel, the pressure you put on the inside shapes the outside of the pot. But it's also the inside of the person—how he feels when he's throwing—that makes a pot what it is.
—Sid Oakley, owner of Cedar Creek Gallery, Creedmoor, North Carolina

1. Potters used to dig their own clay, but because preparation (digging, spreading, drying, washing, and sieving) is so laborious, many craftspeople now use precleansed clays. First, it's weighed—a mug requires about a pound of clay; a teapot 2½ to 3 pounds.

2. The clay is wedged, a slicing and kneading process that removes air pockets.

3. The potter "throws," or shapes, the weighed-and-wedged clay on a revolving wheel.

4. Time for the kiln, which is fueled with electricity, gas, coal, oil, or wood. Most pottery goes through a preliminary "bisque firing," in which it's placed in the kiln and cooked at 1800 degrees for eight to nine hours.

5. The pots are now dry, strong, and thus easily handled and ready for decorating. A "slip" (a dousing of clay, water, and chemical oxides) adds a color base to the pot, then the potter may or may not use a brush or syringe to add a design.

6. A dip in the "glaze," such as an alkaline or feldspathic, seals the porousness of the pot and adds glossy character besides. The bottom of the pot is wiped off to keep it from sticking to the kiln shelf.

7. The kiln is stoked for a second firing, this time at about 2300 degrees for twelve to fifteen hours.

These methods vary from pot to pot. For example, Southern folk potters were less likely to do a bisque firing, and the decoration/glaze was simply and quickly accomplished by throwing salt in the kiln during the firing. But then again, that's the beauty of pottery—no two pieces are alike. Not only will the potter's hands produce a slight variation with every piece, the fire will have its own way.

gallery. They look like brick furnaces, blackened on the inside, littered all around the outside with broken remnants of pots.

But the kilns don't get fired up until Brad's or Sid's or one of the other resident's shelves are full. So it's time to follow the path back to the gallery, where the labyrinthine layout and the pots slow you down to a shuffle, draw you in for a closer look, and invite you to touch. Squat little mugs, gilded in indigo, stacked in careless pairs. A graceful teapot and its brother, a lidded casserole, both speckled and earthy. Porcelain vases and platters so rich and delicate, it's hard to imagine them in the fiery depths of a kiln.

Meanwhile, Sid can be spotted actually giving one of his prized creations—the fragile and notoriously difficult-to-make crystalline-glaze pots that have made him famous—to an Argentine tourist barely old enough for school. When Sid realizes he's been observed, he just mumbles something about the boy giving him Spanish lessons. For now, the moment is lost on the little boy, but someday he'll appreciate his pot from North Carolina —made even more valuable by the memory of the light-haired potter with the black framed glasses who gave it to him.

*E*ven though most pottery is mainly utilitarian, designed for storing food, churning butter, or watering plants, great attention is paid to decoration.

SOUTHERN GARDENS

From the weedy kudzu to the poetic wisteria, Southern plant life is not always different from the greenery of other parts of the country. The region shares its most common garden flowers and many of its trees, for example, with the Northeast and Middle West. And yet, it is easy for a Southerner to assume that lush lawns and rose gardens are distinctly ours.

That's because many of us grew up with yardwork ethics. Lawnmowing and clipping fall right behind death and taxes in importance in the average Southern household. In fact, according to Southern Magazine, *Southerners spend more than four billion dollars a year on*

*W*hat could be more Southern than this country lane overhung with Spanish moss, near Natchez, Mississippi (page 98)? Traditional dogwood and boxwood gardens (this page, top) and the plantation house (bottom) at the Berkeley Plantation, James River, Charles City, Virginia; a colorful Southern tulip garden in spring (page 101).

©Jim Schaefer

lawns and gardens. Thirty-three percent of us have flower gardens, twenty-eight percent of us have vegetable gardens. Even if we don't have a vegetable garden, we can usually count on a relative or neighbor to supply home-grown produce. On vacation or school outings, a national forest or public garden is likely to be included on the itinerary—after all, we've got plenty of them, too.

Besides, for every flower or tree we share with other Americans, there's another that's firmly rooted in our culture. The large, white bloom of the magnolia tree, for example, is synonymous with the South. It's been used to describe our most attractive women as well as our proverbial view of looking at the region through rose-colored glasses. There are six chapters of The Azalea Society of America in the South— and though there certainly are azaleas in other parts of the country, where else would you go to witness a springtime festival honoring the colorful shrub? Camellias, rhododendrons, cypress, dogwoods, collard greens, okra—they all conjure up an image that's vividly us. And we not only don't mind, we're rolling up our sleeves and carting out the wheelbarrow to keep the image alive.

©Steve Knight/Transparencies

The azaleas at Callaway Gardens, in Pine Mountain, Georgia, are among the South's most visited. When the time is right in the spring, the grounds burst with a spectrum of color.

CALLAWAY GARDENS

About halfway down Georgia's western side, where Atlanta is seventy miles north and Alabama is less than an hour's drive, a dream is flourishing. Azaleas spring to life in April, magnolias sweeten the days of July, and the evergreen that gave Pine Mountain its name rules the year-round. Although Cason Callaway has been gone since 1961, the natural beauty that he sought to preserve and enhance is more than alive and well.

The story is pleasant enough. In 1930, this successful textiles entrepreneur from LaGrange took his family south a few miles to Blue Spring, where he fell in love with the foliage and peaceful pace. By 1952 Cason and his wife, Virginia, had not only established a home, progressive farm, and an abundance of plant life at Blue Spring, they'd also created and opened a public garden nearby.

Today, to say the gardens are even more pleasant than the story is an understatement. The plants native to the area are the stars of the show, from the *Azalea prunifolia*, the rare wildflower plum leaf that first inspired Cason to buy Blue Spring, to the dogwoods that seem to salt the woods. Here's a mini-tour.

©Sylvia Martin

The beautiful blossom of the magnolia tree extends its large, snowy petals over rich, dark-green leaves. Adding to its charm is the sweet scent of the flowers.

Laurel Springs Trail

The mountain laurel is a broadleaf evergreen shrub with glossy leaves and umbels of rose-colored or white flowers, and it is here that some of Callaway's prettiest are encouraged to thrive. The woodlands along the secluded slopes of Pine Mountain Ridge and the edge of Laurel Springs Creek also play host to the longleaf Georgia pine, the cinnamon oak, the sweet gum, and other Southern hardwoods.

Meadowlark Gardens

On the Wildflower Trail, Georgia's beauties are at their peak in March, among them Cherokee roses (the state flower), daisies, Japanese honeysuckles, and violets. More than 450 varieties of holly-bearing fruits color the Holly Trail, while the leathery-leaved evergreen blooms on the Rhododendron Trail in the spring. Finally, the fragrant, white-flowered, dark-green-leaved magnolia tree of Southern fame is highlighted in a formal garden in this area.

Azalea Trails

When they bloom in the spring, species of the native Southern azaleas range in color from white to yellow, orange, scarlet, and crimson. Only a few other plants are as popularly associated with the South as this deciduous shrub, a member of the genus *Rhododendron*, and many cities honor it annually. But among the finest tributes is Callaway's own Azalea Trails, where more than seven hundred varieties bloom from late March to May.

PICKING WILDFLOWERS

Don't remove flowers from roadsides or parks. Get the owner's permission to pick from private land.

Choose from abundant populations —not more than a third of any variety. Leave some of the stems to produce seed; don't remove all the blossoms from a single plant.

Flowers are freshest in the early morning or late evening.

Use scissors or pruning shears. Don't tear the flowers from the plant.

Immediately put cut flowers in water or wet paper towel.

At home, recut stems at an angle with sharp scissors. For heavy stems, peel off the last 2 inches of skin. For flowers with a milky secretion, seal the stem tip by momentarily holding over a flame.

To prevent algae from forming, add a few drops of bleach to the vase water.

GARDENS

SOUTHERN AZALEAS

NAME	GENUS	COLOR	GROWS	BLOOMS
Florida	Rhododendron austrinum	golden yellow	West Virginia to Texas	late March, early April
Piedmont	Rhododendron canescens	pure white to deep pink	West Virginia to Texas	late March, early April
Oconee	Rhododendron speciosum	salmon, yellow, orange	West Virginia to mid-Texas	early to mid-April
Pinxter bloom	Rhododendron nudiflorum	white to pale pink, violet-red	Montana to South Carolina	mid-April
Roseshell	Rhododendron roseum	pink	Montana to South Carolina	mid-April
Pinkshell	Rhododendron vaseyi	pink with green throat, orange dots	Montana to South Carolina	mid-April
Alabama	Rhododendron alabamense	pure white or white with yellow or pink cast	West Virginia to mid-Texas	mid to late April
Coastal	Rhododendron alanticum	pure white or white with yellow or pink cast	West Virginia to mid-Texas	mid to late April
Swamp	Rhododendron viscosum	white to pinkish white	Montana to Georgia	mid-May to early June
Flame	Rhododendron calendulaceum	cream to red	Parts of Washington to Georgia	early May to late June
Sweet	Rhododendron arboescens	white to pink	Massachusetts to mid-Texas	early May to late June
Cumberland	Rhododendron bakeri	orange to red	Massachusetts to mid-Texas	late June to early July
Hammock sweet	Rhododendron serulatum	white to creamy	Maryland to mid-Texas	late July to early August
Plumleaf	Rhododendrum prunifolium	orange to fire-red	West Virginia to Texas	July to early September

The Sawyer yard is dark with mulberry trees and it is planted with grass and sweet shrubs. Sometimes after the rain you can smell the sweet shrub all the way into our house; and in the center of the yard there is a sundial which Mrs. Sawyer installed in 1912 as a memorial to her Boston bull, Sunny, who died after having lapped up a bucket of paint."
—Truman Capote,
"Children on
Their Birthdays"

108

©Sylvia Martin

©Sylvia Martin

How to Plant and Care for an Azalea

1. The time to plant is from early fall to early spring, but when the temperatures are above freezing.

2. Be sure to buy from an established and reputable nursery. Unless the plants receive special treatment for a year or two, they are unlikely to survive.

3. Make sure the species will adapt to your climate. The "Rhodora" (Rhododendron canadense), for example, is cold-hardy enough to survive as far north as Minnesota, whereas the "Hammock-Sweet" (Rhododendron serrulatum) is only happy in the region from Virginia to Texas.

4. Depending on the number of azaleas you plan to culture, it's possible to have blooms from late March until August. Piedmonts (Rhododendron canescens), for example, bloom in very early spring whereas the flame azalea (Rhododendron calendulaceum) flowers in summer and the "Pinkshell" (Rhododendron vaseyi) in between.

5. Choose a partly shady spot; avoid windy, exposed areas. A slightly acidic soil, ranging in pH between 5 to 6, is best. The earth should be loose and contain an abundance of humus or well-decomposed matter. Additional organic matter such as peat moss or compost may be required for sandy or loamy soils.

6. Dig a hole one and a half to two times the diameter of the earth ball. Don't dig too deep, as most azaleas are shallowrooted. In fact, it's best to firm the soil at the bottom of the hole and plant high to avoid settling.

7. Remove the plant carefully from the container. If the roots are earth-balled, remove the burlap. Or, cut from the top of the ball after placing in the hole.

8. Water the plant immediately. Afterward, it's important to prevent the soil from becoming soggy or dry. Unless rains are frequent, water about once a week throughout the first growing season.

9. Spacing of the plants varies. Varieties that grow as high as 10 to 12 feet should be planted up to 6 to 8 feet apart; lower types about 3 to 4 feet apart.

10. Mulch is an important part of culture and aftercare. Top the soil with 2 to 4 inches of pine needles, pine bark, coarse peat moss, leaf mold, or other mulches. Replenish as needed, especially during the summer, to reduce evaporation.

11. Newly planted azaleas with a soil high in organic matter often do not need additional fertilizer. However, plants that could benefit should be treated in the spring, just after new growth starts. Commercial azalea fertilizers are available at nurseries. Be sure to water the plants well afterward. A second application can be applied in late June or early July—or add very small amounts 1 month apart.

12. Occasional pruning may be necessary to remove old or weak branches, to encourage new growth, or to shape, and to work the plants into the landscape. Follow the normal growth form of the plant.

*A*zalea displays and festivals are common throughout the South and have become an important resource for luring tourists.

John A. Sibley Horticultural Center

Named for a long-standing member of Callaway's board of trustees, this greenhouse-garden complex features cultivated as well as native plants, working in harmony with nature to provide floral displays all year long. Among the seasonal specialties that have a chance to shine are: the fall-festive chrysanthemums in dramatic cascades, hanging baskets, and flower beds; Christmas poinsettia, interspersed with chrysanthemums, "Paper-White" narcissus, cyclamen, and blue coleus; the caladiums, geraniums, and *Clerodendrons* of June and July; and the pansies and amaryllis of winter.

Mr. Cason's Vegetable Garden

Based on the agricultural techniques developed by Cason Callaway on his Blue Springs Farms, this garden is seven and a half acres of the South's best fruits, vegetables, and herbs. But the garden may be most famous for its muscadine grapes. This native Southern fruit is sweet, dull-purple in color (except the "Scuppernong" variety, which is bronze) and grows in small clusters.

Golf courses, bike paths, a mountain lake, a butterfly conservatory—even the nonhorticultural facilities at this twenty-five-hundred-acre resort are rich with redbuds, daylilies, beautyberries, tea olive, and other plants of this land. Southerners have always had a passion for life—but it took a couple from LaGrange, Georgia, to display some of our best examples for the world to see.

You can visit the John A. Sibley Horticultural Center at any time of the year and see an abundance of colorful flowers, and other plants, indoors and out.

111

©Paul G. Beswick, Courtesy of Callaway Gardens

Dried Flowers

Different flowers require different drying methods. Southern plants that actually dry out and get stiff as they grow, such as goldenrod and butterfly weed, are best air-dried. Flowers that naturally wilt, such as black-eyed susans, dogwoods, roses, daisies, pansies, and lilies, usually need treatment.

The light-colored flowers will retain their color best, whereas the darker ones, especially red, seem to fade. Cut at the height of maturity (except goldenrod, which should be cut before a lot of yellow shows since flowers continue to open as they dry). Pick flowers for drying at noon on a hot, dry day, when the morning dew has dried. Process immediately before wilting begins. A droopy flower can be revived, however, by placing the stems in water for a while. In colonial days, there were always bunches of different harvested flowers hanging from the beams by the fireplace. You, too, can add charm to your own home while you wait, but be sure the area is cool, dry, dimly lit, and well-ventilated. A carport, garage, attic, or any air-conditioned room is ideal for air-drying. You also have the option of drying by artificial means.

113

*M*any of the South's favorite flowers, both wild and cultivated, lend themselves well to drying. How many of these can you identify?

114

GARDENS

Air-drying

1. *After picking, strip the foliage from the stems. Gather into small bunches so the center will dry easily. Tie at the cut end of the stems with rubberbands to keep the flowers from slipping as they shrink.*

2. *Hang upside down to keep the stems straight, making sure the bundles don't touch. The bunches may be hung from a wire hanger, from nails driven into a beam, or pinned to a clothesline strung across the room.*

3. *Allow to dry for 2 or 3 weeks; the flowers with the most moisture will take longest. Dried plants may be sprayed with a clear matte varnish to further preserve them. Arrange several varieties together in a vase or basket, or use them to make a wreath.*

Chemical-drying

1. *You'll need silica gel (available at hobby and flower shops) and a shoebox or plastic container. Fill the box with 1 inch of the chemical. Cut the stems short, then lay a few flowers on the gel, making certain they don't touch each other.*

2. *Slowly sprinkle the gel all around the flowers. As you completely cover them, arrange them so they keep their natural shapes; don't squash them flat with the powdery substance. Dry as many flowers as you have room for.*

3. *Cover the container and seal it so that no moisture can get in. Within 5 days, check the flowers to see if they are ready. They will feel crisp when dry. If not, bury them again.*

4. *When they are dry, remove the flowers and blow away the gel. If the stems had to be cut short, replace them with wire stems that are available in hobby and florist shops. You may further protect them by spraying on a clear varnish or hairspray. Or, keep them in a covered glass container. Remember that direct sunlight will cause the color to fade.*

The Ten Most Common Lawn Flowers

©Sylvia Martin

Begonias

The flowers have a waxy appearance and vary in color from pink to deep red, with one flower often displaying several shades. Begonias are best grown in a cool summer climate or in the shade.

Chrysanthemums

These beautiful flowers are fall bloomers and are among the easiest garden plants to grow. Chrysanthemums usually grow in clusters and range in color from white or yellow to pink or red.

Geraniums

Because they adapt readily to varied conditions, geraniums are widely popular. Their red, pink, or white flowers bloom in large, ball-like clusters during the summer.

Marigolds

Like most of these cultivated flowers, marigolds aren't limited to the South. But home gardeners frequently choose its yellows, oranges, or reds to add color to flower beds.

Petunias

Most petunias are perennials, but they're grown as annuals because they flower during the first summer. Gardeners value them for their large, velvety, funnel-shaped flowers, which vary in hue.

Poppies

Admired for their delicate beauty and gracefulness, poppies are long-lasting flowers in various shades of yellow, rosepink, and scarlet. They bloom in August.

©Derek Fell

Peonies

In late spring, peonies bloom with large red, pink, or white flowers.

©Grant Heilman

Pictured here from left to right: begonias, prized for their textured, multicolored foliage and attractive flowers; peonies, with their leafy shoots and large, handsome blossoms; roses of the climbing and rambler variety, trained on a trellis. Next page: a garden pathway framed by azaleas, rhododendrons and dogwoods.

117

Roses

They don't grow as well here as on the Pacific coast, and yet many Southern lawns feature breathtaking exhibits. For the dozens of varieties, there are dozens of shades and blooming duedates.

Red sage

Also known as salvia or scarlet sage, this soft-haired perennial grows naturally along the roadsides in the coastal plain from South Carolina to Texas but may also be cultivated among the other garden favorites.

Zinnias

A native of Mexico and the Southwest, yet zinnias adapt well to the warm southern climate. Along with the marigold, these flowers are among the most successful of summer annuals. Colors range from red, scarlet, crimson, and pink to salmon, yellow, and bronze.

118

GARDENS

119

*A*mong the lovely sights at the Orton Plantation in Wilmington, North Carolina, is a springtime azalea display (top) and a towering old oak tree (bottom).

120

© Grant Heilman

SOUTHERN TREES

Trees have deep roots in Southern culture. The tall oaks of both Tara and her beloved Ashley's home were a source of great pride and comfort to Scarlett O'Hara. On the other hand, it was "the enormous tree, the fragrant chinaberry tree," that crushed a woman's husband to death and caused her sorrow in Eudora Welty's story "A Curtain of Green."

Trees don't just stir the souls of literary figures. The scented green of Southern pines seems to permeate our memories of camping and Christmas. In more than one childhood reminiscence, there's a walnut tree hung with an old tire for a swing. The oaks and willows planted at new Southern homes—infantile for years, then giant-size by the time a family moves on— are as sentimentally significant as the house itself.

From the fragile-looking mimosa to the sturdy hickory, Southern trees are as regionally renowned as fried chicken, whittling, and plantations. Here's a bird's-eye view of some of the classics.

121

BOXWOOD

Two species of this evergreen are frequently discovered on our soils. Buxus sempervirens, the common box, is featured in the gardens of Williamsburg and Mount Vernon as well as in the more modest lawns of the upper South. Buxus microphylla, from Japan, is prominent in the warmer areas of the Gulf states.

The boxwood thrives in well-drained, sandy, loamy soils high in organic matter and with a pH between 5.5 and 7. Semishade— not full sun and dry, hot areas— works best. Plant shallowly and mulch with pine needles or other organic materials; cultivating around the shrubs can destroy their root systems.

Water until the soil is thoroughly wet, but avoid planting near drain spouts. Prune annually during the first several years after it's planted, until the shrub reaches the desired sizes, then prune periodically. Be sure to remove dead branches to help prevent disease-causing fungi. Fertilize in the early spring, and if need be, again in early June. The fertilizer should not come within six inches of the boxwood's main stem.

The Oaks

Though the fifty-four native American oaks aren't limited to the South (they're in the Northeast too), many figure prominently in its regional identity and history. Southern oaks stand as monuments to battles fought on the grounds, from the Revolutionary War to the Civil War. The United States Navy built its first frigate, the *Constitution*, from live oak cut from trees on St. Simons Island, Georgia. And all too many Southerners met their deaths from being hung from oaks when the law was scarce.

Oaks are divided in two groups, white and black. The white oak, named for its light, ashy-gray bark, reaches heights of 80 to 100 feet with a trunk diameter of 2 to 4 feet. Its leaves usually have seven to nine fingerlike rounded lobes, which turn wine or russet red in the fall. Superb examples of evergreen live oak grow on old plantations near Savannah. The swamp chestnut, which grows along Southern creeks and riverbanks, and Durand's, which is particularly abundant around Albany, Georgia, are other types of white oak.

The Black Oaks are easy to identify, for on older trees the bark is nearly black. When it's grown, the black oak averages about 70 or 80 feet with a trunk diameter of 1 to 3 feet. The leaves have bristle-tipped lobes. It's found throughout the South from the mountains to the coast, but it's most common in the lower mountains. Two of the South's most popular shade trees, the Southern red oak and the willow oak, grow about 70 feet tall and have rounded canopies. Both number among the black oaks.

© Grant Heilman

© Grant Heilman

In rural areas, bark from red oaks (opposite page) has been used to make a medicinal tea. The Georgia pine (this page) is among the evergreens that comprise the "pine belt," a vast forestland stretching from the Carolinas to Texas.

The Pines

Eleven species of pine are found in the South, and the loblolly is one of the most common. This large tree which grows as high as 170 feet is abundant in the coastal plain and eastern piedmont of Virginia and North Carolina and throughout most of South Carolina, Georgia, and southeastern Tennessee. The beautiful white pine, with its delicate bluish-green needles, is just as common in the North; however, it extends as far South as northeastern Georgia and is most at home in mountainous Southern areas. Cedar, also known as juniper, is among the county's oldest living trees, plus the wood is important to the regional furniture industry. Finally, the short-leaf, slash, longleaf, and Carolina hemlocks are commonly associated with the South.

© Grant Heilman

Flowering Trees

Even more famous than the flowering fruit trees are the dogwoods and magnolias. The dogwood grows wild throughout most of the region, and yet Southerners strive to cultivate more. It's no wonder, since the tree is a year-round spectacle. In winter, the dogwood's bare branches are tipped with silvery pearls. In spring, the pearls are transformed into a mass of white or red blooms and glossy, grayish-green leaves. Festivals throughout the South, such as the ones in Atlanta and Knoxville, Tennessee, attest to the popularity of this particular event and in fall, the leaves burst into vivid scarlet.

There are many forms of magnolias, but our finest and best-known is the Southern magnolia, "one of those plants that Southerners grew up with and Northerners would die for," according to *Southern Living*. The exquisite waxy flowers of white that bloom in late spring are among the largest (6 to 8 inches wide) and most fragrant of any tree. Compared to the Southern magnolia, which can grow up to 100 feet in height, the sweet bay or swamp magnolia is considerably smaller, between 15 and 70 feet. Its flowers are smaller as well, about 2 to 3 inches wide but are no less fragrant or lovely and they continue to bloom through spring and summer. Magnolias are native from North Carolina to Texas. Louisiana purportedly has the most impressive examples of the Southern magnolia, while the south-eastern coastal plain lays claim to the prettiest sweet bay magnolias.

© Grant Heilman

The flowering trees of the South are closely identified with the imagery of the region. Pictured on the opposite page are redbuds and dogwoods. On this page: a flowering pear tree.

There are other flowering wonders where those came from. April in Alabama brings the small, pea-blossom shaped, rose-purple flower of the redbud. The tulip tree has spring blossoms that resemble its namesake, except they're only 1 to 2 inches across and the petals are greenish yellow with orange bands across the base. The pale pink, purple-tinged blossoms of the chinaberry were brought to the United States from India, whereas the feathery whites, yellows, and reds of the mimosa originated from Persia. But now, both of these unusual trees are firmly rooted in Dixie.

The Fruit Trees

Apples, peaches, figs, cherries, and plums all grow in the South, and some are just as cherished for their spring flowers as their summer fruits. The fragrant, deep-pink blossoms of the apple tree, so similar to those of the wild rose, draw flocks of admirers to Winchester, Virginia. The blossoms of the peach tree are also pink and showy, but they're most popular in Georgia's inlands and South Carolina's central and western areas. The river plum tree puts on a show in Chapel Hill, North Carolina, and the chickasaw plum springs to life in Kentucky. In the autumn, the wild plum thickets are a mosaic of bronze from Kentucky southward, while the black cherry turns a bright golden yellow in the Allegheny Mountains from West Virginia to Alabama.

© Grant Heilman

POTTED PALMS

Not all of us are lucky enough to live in the Southern coastal states or to have a lawn of our own. But you can enjoy a little bit of the southernmost coasts by keeping a potted palm indoors. Most palms are too large to use as houseplants, but the pygmy palm and the parlor palm are exceptions.

Although the pygmy eventually reaches heights of 12 feet, it requires several years to form a trunk. It grows best in diffused light, with an eastern exposure and morning sun. The parlor palm, on the other hand, grows rapidly to about 8 feet tall and prefers dim light. Consequently, it's ideal to place against an inside wall.

The potting soil mix for both palms should consist of one part peat moss, one part garden loam, and one part sand. In the summer, keep soil evenly moist; in the winter, allow the soil to become dry to the touch before watering. Sponge the leaves with a damp cloth weekly. Maintain the temperature between 76 to 78 degrees. Large tubs are ideal for palms; repot every few years.

Other Special Trees

The sweet gum and black gum are not related to each other, and yet they're both noted for their fall foliage. The sweet gum, a massive tree with light gray bark, positively blazes with yellows, oranges, reds, and bronzes. The black gum or sour gum, the smaller of the two, turns a brilliant scarlet with purple or orange.

The Atlantic coastal plain and the Gulf and Mississippi valley are rich with the historical cypress trees. According to the Bible, Noah's ark was built of cypress ("gopher wood"), and now this thin-barked, narrow-leaved tree is a familiar Southern sight, particularly in Louisiana and Mississippi.

Finally, there are palmettos on the shores of North Carolina, South Carolina, and Georgia. The largest Southern hardwood, the widely abundant sycamore, sheds its bark to expose a whitish wood. And the festive American holly, which reaches its greatest size in the rich bottomlands of southern Arkansas, also adds color to the landscape.

© Lefever-Grushow/Grant Heilman

One of the South's
most noted
types of hardwoods,
a black gum in Tupelo,
Mississippi (far left);
various magnolias
(left); and an American
sycamore (bottom).
Next page: the beloved
and celebrated live oak,
as tenacious as it is
stately.

© Grant Heilman

KUDZU

*This weedy vine might have
Japanese roots, but in America it's
pure and simply Southern. Not
only does kudzu cover two million
acres of forestland in the South, it
has assumed almost mythical
cultural significance.*

*First introduced to the South
through the Japanese pavilion
at the 1884 New Orleans
Exposition, kudzu was adopted for
its ability to shade porches and to
control erosion. Now categorized
as a weed, this fast-growing, large-
leaf vine threatens the lives of trees
by enveloping them and shutting
out the sun.*

*Yet, for its horticultural
ordinariness, you might say
kudzu occupies a special place in
the heart of Dixie. Kudzu queens
have been crowned; newspapers,
comic strips, and rock bands have
been named for it; and most every
Southern writer has mentioned the
imposing plant at least once.*

STATE	NICKNAME	ORIGIN
Alabama	Camellia State	Named for a Native American tribe called *Alabamas* or *Alibamos*, of the Creek Confederacy.
Georgia	Peach State	Named for King George II of England.
Kentucky	Bluegrass State	A Native American word, translated variously as "dark and bloody ground," "meadow land," and "land of tomorrow," was the basis of this state's name.
Louisiana	Pelican State	Part of a territory called *Louisiana*, after King Louis XIV of France.
Mississippi	Magnolia State	Probably from the Chippewa words, *mici zibi*, meaning "great river," or "gathering in all the waters."
North Carolina	Tar Heel State	Originally a province called Carolana, the name derived from *Carolus*, which is Latin for Charles. The province was granted by King Charles I to Sir Robert Heath in 1619.
South Carolina	Palmetto State	Same as for North Carolina. The province was split into North and South Carolina after a new patent was granted by Charles II to the Earl of Clarendon.
Tennessee	Volunteer State	*Tanasi* was the name of Cherokee villages on the Little Tennessee river. (Tennessee was called Franklin, or Frankland, between 1784 and 1788.)
Virginia	Old Dominion	Named by Sir Walter Raleigh, who fitted out the expedition of 1584, in honor of Queen Elizabeth, The Virgin Queen of England.
West Virginia	Mountain State	Named when the western counties of Virginia refused to secede from the U.S. in 1863.

128

FLOWER	BIRD	TREE
Camellia	Yellowhammer	Southern Pine
Cherokee Rose	Brown Thrasher	Live Oak
Goldenrod	Cardinal	Kentucky Coffee Tree
Magnolia	Eastern Brown Pelican	Cypress
Magnolia	Mockingbird	Magnolia
Dogwood	Cardinal	Pine
Carolina Jessamine	Carolina Wren	Palmetto
Iris	Mockingbird	Tulip Popular
Dogwood	Cardinal	Dogwood
Big Rhododendron	Cardinal	Sugar Maple

GARDENS

MR. BOYER AND THE LAST OF THE ROADSIDE VENDORS

"I want you to pick all the fruit this year and see that nothing is wasted. There's always someone who can use it. Don't let good things rot for want of using. You waste life when you waste good food."
—Katherine Ann Porter, "The Jilting of Granny Weatherall," Flowering Judas and Other Stories

Imagine a Southern summer without these men of little words and their bushels and crates and makeshift stands. It's hard to imagine our children not having a Mr. Boyer.

Oh, there are some left. Like the skinny old man who parks his truck on the abandonded drive-in parking lot, then moves his chair to the shade to wait for customers. I don't know much about him, except that he lives "yonder past them trees" and he's always throwing in an extra tomato for free.

Mr. Boyer wasn't any different from the other old-timers who sell their fruits and vegetables from a truck on the side of the road. You couldn't say we knew him well, either. We figured he was religious, since he was nowhere to be seen on Sundays. But then again, a lot of Southerners, especially the older ones, still don't work on the Lord's day. We knew that he had a real nice wife, lived in a neat little house, and he wore a hat and overalls—little things like that. But you couldn't really say we knew Mr. Boyer.

It was sad, nevertheless, when we read his obituary. We didn't know his first name, but the address gave him away. He was getting on, you could tell, and his truck hadn't been parked out in the driveway in quite a while. His garden hadn't looked too spry, either. I guess you could say we saw it coming—whatever "it" was, the newspaper didn't say—but the realization of the thing was sobering. Not only because this man had an obituary full of people who were going to miss him, but because we're losing altogether too many Mr. Boyers. His breed of crusty old farmers is shipping out, and they're taking their homegrown science with them.

Time was when there were younger generations to pick up where the older farmers left off. Now we've got condos and Hondas instead of acres, and educations instead of green thumbs. But will a supermarket tomato ever taste as full of life? It's sad to think of children growing up in families that don't have a vegetable gardener.

We had one in ours. To him, a garden was as essential to a backyard as roosters were to dawn. So even after he sold his big farm in the 1950's, he continued to till the land that came with his little wooden houses. As he aged, the gardens became smaller and smaller, but the goods were no less succulent. Even we children could appreciate the just-picked quality of his corn, cucumbers, and cantaloupe. It didn't have anything to do with nutrition or economics—we just liked the taste.

In fact, he paid us little attention except for when it came to the garden. A second helping of okra or summer squash won us a smile and a "Good, ain't they?" When our visit was up, his goodbye usually came in the form of, "Go out there in the garden and get what you want. Ain't no sense in it going to waste." And when he had planted his last garden, the way he remembered us was by the stories he repeated over and over—about how one of us helped him plow when we were only ya-high, about how another helped him tie up tomato plants, lickety-split. And on and on.

So now he's gone, and Mr. Boyer's gone, and any number of men who knew string beans better than their own grandkids are gone. It might not be long before every day is Sunday.

133

Our Favorite Garden Plants

Here's a rundown of the fruits and vegetables that grace our gardens, not to mention our tables, every season:

*T*he raising of vegetables and fruits in small garden plots is a continuing tradition in the modern South (page 136). Pictured here from left to right: sugar beets, okra, and sweet potatoes.

Beets

A familiar sight on Southern supper tables is pickled slices of dark red beet roots. They grow almost trouble-free and may be harvested all summer. Planting should take place as early in spring as the ground can be worked.

Cantaloupe

Also known as muskmelons, cantaloupes grow on vines during the warm season. When the cantaloupe takes on a rich color and partly separates from the stem, it's ready for harvesting.

Corn

Most of America's corn is grown in the Midwest, but Southerners are partial to their own. Farmers plant corn in early spring and harvest in late summer.

Collard Greens

This relative of the cabbage is usually limited to the gardens of the South, since it grows well in warm climates and is a strong member of Dixie food culture. In very warm climates, the seeds may be planted in September and the leaves picked the following spring and summer. Or the seeds may be planted in summer and picked the following winter.

Cucumbers

The cucumber plant is a vine with a hairy stem that grows well in warm weather. If they're harvested as soon as they're 2 to 3 inches long, the plants will produce cucumbers all year long.

Okra

This prickly, spear-shaped pod belongs to the South, since Northerners have never figured out how to cook it. The plants grow to heights of 2 to 8 feet and should be harvested in midsummer, a few days after the flowers fall and when the pods are 2 to 4 inches long.

Potatoes

New potatoes from the supermarket never taste as good as the ones from a local garden. The edible part of the plant is actually attached to underground stems.

String Beans

Also known as snap beans, string beans are a member of the pea family. They're picked when they're very young—usually in the spring, before they have a chance to fully ripen—to become dry beans.

© Grant Heilman

Sweet Potatoes

The sweet potato isn't a true potato—it's a vine related to the morning glories. The vegetable plant is grown from roots in greenhouses, and removed and planted, then harvested before frost in the fall. The South—especially Louisiana, North Carolina, and Virginia—is the leading producer of the sweet potato, which likes warm, moist, sandy soil.

Tomatoes

Although they're not hard to grow, gardeners start with six- to eight-week-old plants from greenhouses. Planting begins about two weeks after the last frost of spring. Tying the stalks to posts keeps tomatoes from spoiling on the moist ground under the plant's heavy foliage.

Watermelon

The few fruits that the watermelon vine produces are large—averaging 20 to 35 pounds. The seeds should not be planted until the heat of summer. The vines grow to be about 12 to 15 feet long. The melons require eighty to ninety days for ripening. Georgia and South Carolina are among the leading producers.

Yams

Although not related to the sweet potato, the roots of this tropical plant are similar. The "yams" we have in America, however, are not really yams at all but especially juicy varieties of sweet potatoes. The misconception apparently originated with the Southern slaves, who had lived on the real thing in their native land and called sweet potatoes by the African word "to eat" (*njam*, *nyami*, or *djambi*).

Yellow Squash

This summer vine grows rapidly and the fruits are harvested before they mature, at about 3 to 6 inches long. The seeds are planted in hills (groups of about three plants) about two weeks before the last frost of spring.

THE GARDENS OF THE SLAVES

In the antebellum South, slaves were forced to work for their masters five to six days a week. But at the end of the workday and on Sundays, some were allowed to tend their gardens.

The patches supplemented the workers' meager rations of food. The gardens occasionally provided spending money as well—some masters purchased produce from their slaves or allowed them to market the goods in town as an incentive to work.

The West African influence can be seen in Southern gardens today. Although not necessarily a widespread practice, mixing the plant types together, rather than separating them into precise rows, is a carryover from the gardens of the slaves. (The theory behind this type of gardening is that layering plants next to each other reduces the insect population and conserves water.) What's more, the vegetables that distinguish Southern gardens from those of other Americans—yams, okra, and collards, for example—are the very ones brought by the slaves from their own homeland.

136

GARDENS

138

Homes

Historic houses that offer lodging:

Madewood Plantation House
Route 2, Box 478
Napoleonville, LA 70390

The Myrtles Plantation
Highway 61
P.O. Box 1100
St. Francisville, LA 70775-1100

Historic houses to visit:

Destrehan Plantation
9999 River Road
Destrehan, LA 70047

Houmas House Plantation
Route 1, Box 181
Convent, LA 70723

Shadows-on-the-Teche
317 East Main Street
New Iberia, LA 70560

Rosedown Plantation and Gardens
P.O. Box 1816
St. Francisville, LA 70775

Magnolia Plantation and Gardens
Route 4
Charleston, SC 29407

Orton Plantation
Route 1, Box 57
Winnabow, NC 28479

Historic Charleston Foundation
51 Meeting Street
Charleston, SC 29401
Ask for general information or about the annual Festival of Homes during the spring.

The Visitor Information Center
85 Calhoun Street
Charleston, SC
Information is available on a number of private house museums.

Beauregard-Keyes House
1113 Chartres Street
New Orleans, LA 70116

Gallier House Museum
118-23 Royal Street
New Orleans, LA 70116

Hermann-Grima Historic House
820 St. Louis Street
New Orleans, LA 70112

New Orleans Tours and Convention Services, Inc.
7801 Edinburgh Street
New Orleans, 70125
Tour either plantation or New Orleans-style homes.

Thomas Wolfe Memorial
P.O. Box 7143
Asheville, NC 28807

For more information:

New Orleans Jazz and Heritage Festival
1205 N. Rampart
New Orleans, LA

To order books:

Plantations of the Old South
Oxmoor House, Inc.
P.O. Box 2463
Birmingham, AL 35282
Retails for $19.95

Gardens

Gardens to visit:

Callaway Gardens
Pine Mountain, GA 31822

Live Oak Gardens
284 Rip van Winkle Road
New Iberia, LA 70560

Hodges Gardens
P.O. Box 900
Many, LA 71449

North Carolina Botanical Gardens
University of North Carolina–
Chapel Hill
Totten Center, 457A
Chapel Hill, NC 27514

Cypress Gardens
Oakley, SC
c/o Department of Leisure Services
Hampton Park
Charleston, SC 29403

Biltmore House & Gardens
1 North Pack Square
Asheville, NC 28801

To order seeds and plants:

George W. Park Seed Company
Box 31
Greenwood, SC 29647

Brittingham Plant Farms
P.O. Box 2538
Dept. SC
Salisbury, MD 21802

Savage Farm Nursery
P.O. Box 125
McMinnville, TN 37110

Food

To order books:

Southern Wildflowers
Longstreet Press
2150 Newmarket Parkway
Suite 102
Marietta, GA 30067
Book lists for $29.95. Call for
shipping and handling information.

Trees of the Southeastern
United States
University of Georgia Press
Terrell Hall
Athens, GA 30602
Order for $19.95 plus $1.50 shipping
and handling. Georgia residents add
4 percent sales tax.

Successful Southern Gardening:
A Practical Guide for Year-Round
Beauty
University of North Carolina Press
P.O. Box 2288
Chapel Hill, NC 27515-2288
Order for $24.95 (hardback) or
$12.95 (paperback) plus $1.50 postage.

To order barbecue:

Carolina Treet
P.O. Box 1017
Wilmington, NC 28402

Dreamland Bar-B-Q Drive Inn
2518 8th Street
Tuscaloosa, AL 35401
Order ribs or sauce by overnight mail
for between $40 and $170.

Crafts

To order handmade goods:

Dollywood Gifts
700 Dollywood Lane
Pigeon Forge, TN 37863-4101
A pottery jug, Cherokee Indian
Basket, and hand-tied broom are
available. Shipping is extra.

To order craft supplies:

Jo-Belles Inc.
P.O. Box 1038
Conover, NC 28613
Broommaking, pottery, quilting, and
basket supplies available.

To order or rent videotapes:

Appalshop Films
P.O. Box 743
Whitesburg, KY 41858
Tapes available on quilts, hand-
carving, and apple dolls, among
others.

Instructional Media Center
East Tennessee State University
Box 22507A Johnson City, TN
37614
Tapes available on dulcimer- and sled-
makers, among others.

Appendix
(continued)

To order books:

By Southern Hands: A Celebration
of Craft Traditions in the South
Oxmoor House, Inc.
P.O. Box 2463
Birmingham, AL 35282

Turners and Burners: The Folk
Potters of North Carolina
University of North Carolina Press
P.O. Box 2288
Chapel Hill, NC 27515-2288

Southern Highland Handicraft Guild
P.O. Box 9545
Asheville, NC 28815
Available are The New Basket:
A Vessel for the Future, *and*
"We the Quilters," *among others.*

Other Sources

Encyclopedia of Southern Culture
Center for the Study of Southern
Culture
University of Mississippi
University, MS 38677

Southpoint: The Metropolitan
Monthly magazine
P.O. Box 420077
Palm Coast, FL 32142-9840

Southern Accents magazine
P.O. Box 822
Birmingham, AL 35282-9710

Southern Living magazine
P.O. Box 830119
Birmingham, AL 35282-9848

Division of the Arts
c/o Louisiana Crafts Program
Dept. LTPA
P.O. Box 44247
Baton Rouge, LA 70804
Sourcebook of crafts and the people
who make them is available.

For more information:

Cedar Creek Gallery
Route 2, Box 420
Creedmoor, NC 27522

To order cookbooks:

Famous Recipes from Mrs. Wilkes'
Boarding House in Historic
Savannah
107 West Jones Street
Savannah, GA 31401

The Commander's Palace
New Orleans Cookbook
1403 Washington Avenue
New Orleans, LA 70130

To order New Orleans-style foods:

N'awlins Cajun & Creole Spices
1200 N. Peters Street, Suite 95
New Orleans, LA 70116
Products include gator sausage,
andouille, and cayenne pepper

Café Du Monde
1039 Decatur Street
New Orleans, LA 70116

To order ham:

Gwaltney of Smithfield, Ltd.
P.O. Box 489
Smithfield, VA 23430

For more information:

Louisiana Association of Fairs
and Festivals
Route 3, Box 174
De Ridder, LA 70634
Ask for a free brochure of festivals
honoring Louisiana food and music.

Bibliography

Arnow, Janet. *By Southern Hands: A Celebration of Craft Traditions in the South.* Birmingham (Alabama): Oxmoor House, 1987.

Bailey, Lee. *Lee Bailey's Southern Food and Plantation Houses.* New York: Clarkson N. Potter, 1989.

Bonesteel, Georgia. *Lap Quilting.* Birmingham (Alabama): Oxmoor House, 1982.

Chamberlain, Samuel. *Southern Interiors of Charleston, South Carolina.* New York: Hastings House, 1956.

Curt, Bruce. *Great Houses of New Orleans.* New York: Knopf, 1977.

Duncan, Wilbur H. and Marion B. Duncan. *Trees of the Southeastern United States.* Athens: University of Georgia Press, 1988.

Eanes, Ellen Fickling, et al. *North Carolina Quilts.* Chapel Hill: University of North Carolina Press, 1985.

Eaton, Allen H. *Handicrafts of the Southern Highlands.* New York: Dover Publications Inc., 1973.

Egerton, John. *Southern Food: at Home, on the Road, in History.* New York: Knopf, 1987.

Fraser, Walter J., Jr. *Charleston! Charleston! The History of a Southern City.* Columbia: University of South Carolina Press, 1989.

Hastings, Don. *Gardening in the South.* Dallas: Taylor Publishing Company, 1987.

Hunt, William Lanier. *Southern Gardens, Southern Gardening.* Durham: Duke University Press, 1982.

Ladendorf, Sandra F. *Successful Southern Gardening: A Practical Guide for Year-Round Beauty.* Chapel Hill: The University of North Carolina Press, 1989.

Marshall, Gillian Bertram. *Southern Living's Cooking Across the South, A Collection and Recollection of Favorite Regional Recipes.* Birmingham (Alabama): Oxmoor House, 1980.

Martin, Laura C. *Southern Wildflowers.* Marietta (Georgia): Longstreet Press, 1989.

Mullins, Lisa C., ed. *Early American Southern Homes.* Pittstown (New Jersey): The Main Street Press, 1989.

Neal, Bill. *Southern Cooking.* Chapel Hill: University of North Carolina Press, 1985.

Ramsey, Bets and Merikay Waldovogel. *The Quilts of Tennessee: Images of Domestic Life Prior to 1930.* Nashville; Rutledge Hill Press, 1986.

Ripley, Alexandra. *New Orleans Legacy.* New York: Macmillan, 1987.

Stephenson, Sue H. *Basketry of the Appalachian Mountains.* New York: Prentice Hall Press, 1971.

Sweezy, Nancy. *Raised in Clay.* Washington: Smithsonian Institution Press, 1984.

Tolley, Lynne and Pat Mitchamore. *Jack Daniel's Spirit of Tennessee Cookbook.* Nashville: Rutledge Hill Press, 1988.

Wilson, Charles Reagan and William Ferris, eds. *Encyclopedia of Southern Culture.* Chapel Hill: The University of North Carolina Press, 1989.

Index

INDEX